Karl & Mary,

It's been so much
getting to know you two.
love Well.

Stay Stro...

Michael Gonzales

IF YOU LOVE ME, YOU WILL . . .

*Learning to Love God with All
Your Heart, Soul, and Mind—
and Others as Yourself*

MICHAEL GONZALES

WESTBOW
PRESS*
A DIVISION OF THOMAS NELSON
& ZONDERVAN

WestBow Press books may be ordered through booksellers or by contacting:

WestBow Press
A Division of Thomas Nelson & Zondervan
1663 Liberty Drive
Bloomington, IN 47403
www.westbowpress.com
1 (866) 928-1240

ISBN: 978-1-9736-5041-6 (sc)
ISBN: 978-1-9736-5042-3 (hc)
ISBN: 978-1-9736-5040-9 (e)

Library of Congress Control Number: 2019900096

Print information available on the last page.

WestBow Press rev. date: 1/31/2019

I dedicate this book to God who has changed me at the core where possible and has been merciful in those areas I still may struggle. To my Lord, Savior and best friend Jesus Christ, and His Holy Spirit who continues to teach me how to love like they do. To my wife Linda, who has been my earthly experience of unconditional love and has been there through the hardest parts of those changes. I will forever be grateful for God placing you in my life, loving me, and being patient and committed through it all. The only thing I would change would have been learning how to love you better; sooner. And to all those who have touched my life with their presence. I am sorry for any hurt I may have caused and pray I never repeat it. I look forward to sharing eternity with you all and ask that you, please seek the truth concerning Christ, to make sure this happens.

Contents

Introduction

From Jesus Christ ("If you Love Me, you will keep My commandments" [John 14:15 NASB]) to the woman longing to be valued. From the man trying to manipulate his wife to the child craving chocolate, we hear the words "If you love me, you will ..." Those words have been used to try to establish guidelines within a relationship. Love throughout history has been a means to promote both healthy and unhealthy relationships. Love can be used to encourage and build up or to manipulate and control. It has been used as the battle line to attack and withdraw or as a justification to enable. The lack of understanding of what love truly is in its many forms is the single most destructive force to a relationship of any kind or is the catalyst to a healthier, committed relationship.

My hope in writing this book is to help us all be aware of how we use love to help, hinder, engage in a relationship for the benefit of others or to feed our own selfish needs and desires. The lines aren't always so clear, and the natural outflow of who we are at our core often seeks a hidden agenda that blurs the lines of the most to the least emotionally healthy person. While I am not a licensed therapist, nor do I play one on TV, I have sought to gain understanding from our God and to study many authors who have degrees and have been diligent enough to put their ideas into writing. The ideas in this book are in no way meant to offer therapy or counseling in any manner but only to offer ideas I have learned by living life in and out of the kingdom of God. I have also studied the Greek language under the guidance of a very renowned Greek scholar, Pastor George Westlake, to better mine the intricacies from God's written word. Having served thirteen years as a pastor in a large church and spending many hours offering spiritual guidance, with a focus on addictive behaviors and relationships, I believe God has taught me some ideas about love that can change unhealthy relationships or enhance healthy ones. I have used various versions of the Bible, depending on which one I believed is accurate from the original language and offers the best understanding of the ideas presented. No book could contain the vast amount of understanding of what love truly is, and I don't claim this one to be exhaustive, because love is about life and how it is to be lived out in all of its intricacies. I pray that the ideas in the following pages will help you to "love the Lord your God with all your heart and with all your soul and with all your mind" (Matthew 22:37) and to "love your neighbor as yourself" (Matthew 22:39).

In Christ's love,
Michael Gonzales

CHAPTER 1

What Is Love?

As I began writing this chapter, my fondness for getting into the more profound things—or, as some would put it, getting into the weeds—tugged at me to explain the history of ideas about love and the different ways certain words are interpreted. I wanted to dissect the proper and improper understandings of the word. However, that subject would be a book in itself, and very few would want to read it. So I will save those ideas for friends who like to go to those mind-bending places, and I'll keep the ideas in this book more concise and understandable so more might read and grasp the principles in it.

So let me share what I have learned concerning what love is, and the rest of the book will be more about how it does (and should) play out in life.

I will deal mainly with two basic ideas for love. There are several words the Greeks used for love since their language was very expressive and exact. The reason why God used the Greek language for the New Testament presentation. Here is my understanding of these ideas for love.

Phileo

The most basic meaning of the Greek word *phileo* is a love of the emotions or affections of the heart. This love may be seen in friendships, families (although another word *storge* was explicitly used for natural family affection), and relationships of all kinds. I can have strong emotions or affections toward another person, for a place I like to visit, or for a particular food I enjoy. I can love (phileo) my wife, my friends, Hawaii, ice cream, or, in my case, tacos (although the Greek word *eros* is more specifically about human desires). I think we have all had our heartstrings tugged when watching a child reunited with someone who has been away in service to our country, or a child who has received their first puppy or kitten. The main idea to grasp is that *phileo* is a love that comes from, and guided by the emotions, heart, or desires. It is more a feeling of the heart than a choice of the mind.

Agape

The most basic meaning of the Greek word *agape* would be a love of the mind or will. *Agape* love is seen in relationships of all kinds, but the main idea is that it's a love guided by the mind or will, and it is unconditional in its purest form. It is a love that makes willful choices for the good of others, often involving sacrifice.

Here is an excerpt from *Strong's Exhaustive Concordance* #5368:

> "From philos; to be a friend to (fond of (an individual or an object)), i.e. Have affection for (denoting personal attachment, as a matter of sentiment or feeling; while agapao is wider, embracing especially the judgment and the

deliberate assent of the will as a matter of principle, duty and propriety: the two thus stand related very much as ethelo and boulomai, or as thumos and nous respectively; the former being chiefly of the heart and the latter of the head)."[1]

How is that for staying out of the weeds? I must admit that moving forward is difficult for me without turning the above sentences into a book, but as I said, not many would want to read it. Doing so would probably be more about my need to prove myself than my needing to go into that kind of detail. I understand that there are those who will agree or disagree with some of the ideas I have presented, and I'm okay with that since I love challenges and new ideas. The ideas to follow are merely my current understanding of how I have interpreted God's leading and the circumstances or experiences in my life and ministry—and I love sharing what God has taught me through growth and learning.

So let's talk more about these two ideas of love. Phileo love is more of a natural love for most people. Many don't have in their nature; a heart turned toward others because of how they were taught what love means in their past. Phileo love isn't one I have as much control over since it's more about a feeling. It ebbs and flows, has highs and lows, and basically is what it is at any given moment. Because it's such a natural part of our existence, it seems just to happen—or not happen. We find ourselves feeling it or not feeling it.

Phileo love can be very protective and nurturing, or it can be detrimental to making wise decisions. And while it's a significant part of our being, it must have boundaries around its ability to guide our decision-making. While it's usually part

---

[1] *Strong's Exhaustive Concordance* by James Strong S.T.D., LL.D. 1890 Public Domain.

of our decision-making process, it should never be the lone idea by which we process information, and it should rarely be our primary guide. Our experiences, perceptions, and biases as well as how we have received love from others have highly influenced it.

Agape love, on the other hand, is rarely a natural idea used in decision-making unless one has been raised in an environment of agape love and taught its principles from early on in life. I think you will understand by the end of this book that this scenario would be extremely rare. Agape love says, "I will use my mind and will to try always to do what is best or good for all concerned, even if my heart or emotions may be prompting me to do otherwise." True agape love is the basis for making mature decisions when it comes to responding appropriately to all our relationships.

When both agape and phileo love are present, there is a deep, abiding love. But agape love may or may not contain, or be influenced by, phileo love. Many times, if we practice agape love, phileo love will follow, because the mind's ideas can greatly influence the heart. Agape love can prepare the heart's soil for emotional phileo love, especially when the recipient of our agape love reciprocates that love. Both are necessary and healthy within intimate relationships, but agape love should always take precedence when given the opportunity, meaning there are times when the promptings of the heart are so strong that it may be difficult to allow the mind to go through a process of agape love, though it is usually best. There are times, however, when the prompting of the heart is enough to act relationally healthy, as in times when the safety and well-being of loved ones are concerned.

From Scripture

Here is a scripture that uses both forms of love in the original Greek. "Now about your *love* for one another we do not need to write to you, for you yourselves have been taught by God to *love* each other" (1 Thessalonians 4:9, emphasis added).

The first mention of *love* here uses a form of the word *Philadelphia*, which means "brotherly love." The second mention uses a form of the word *agape.* Let's look closer with this understanding. Paul said that regarding your love for one another, brotherly love—which is a form of phileo or emotional love for one another—isn't something he needed to write about to you. In other words, the emotional love they had for each other came from their hearts, and he didn't even need to discuss it because it's natural and is what it is. But God had taught us (we had to learn it) to have agape love for each other, that love of the mind or will that says, "I will always try to make decisions that are best for others over myself."

You see, agape love is something we learn from God. And while phileo love is natural and from our hearts and emotions, God is still involved in trying to change our hearts. Many scriptures speak of this effort by God to change the desires of our hearts, and it happens in many ways. Just know that while our hearts and emotions, generally speaking, are what they are naturally and experientially, God is still involved in influencing those emotions for our best good and the good of mankind. Godly ideas must influence agape love, or we could easily believe we are doing what is in the best interest of others but be operating from selfish or hurtful places, which can then lead to abusive situations when someone is making decisions from bad agape love ideas or a bad heart. I have also seen people set free from the lies of their pasts by learning what love truly is and is not. There are also those who don't receive something when someone genuinely is trying to do what is best for them. Children and teens often respond from this place when a parent is employing "tough love" in trying to do what is best for them. I have a pet rabbit and two horses, and they can mistake my actions for something they should be afraid of when I'm just trying to help them. People often respond this way based on their experiences of how love has been exhibited to them in the past.

Now let's move on to how these two simple ideas of love play out in extraordinary ways in the life of every human who has or will walk the face of this earth.

CHAPTER 2

God's Ideas of Love

A good friend and mentor of mine, Dr. Paul Carlisle, once taught me one of the most valuable ideas, which God has used to shape my belief system and enhance my relationships of all kinds. Dr. Paul spoke these words to me: "The will cannot choose from ideas the mind does not hold." Please reread and ponder that statement. I hope it will impact your life as it has mine. The concept is that we can operate only from the ideas our minds hold within. These ideas come from different places, with one place being our family environment when we were young, this is called "formation." Those who have studied the psyche (Greek word *psuche* for "soul") understand the importance of this formation in the makeup of who we are at the core. Many good books exist on the topic of formation. Our souls have been taught and have experienced others' ideas of what love is and isn't, and once our souls have come to know something, they can't unknow it. They must then learn new ideas of what true love is to experience and offer it in its intended form; this is sort of like learning a new language. Once learned, it's what you naturally speak and what you know. If you want to speak a different language, you must learn one.

Others also influence our ideas such as extended family members, teachers, friends, good or bad experiences, traumas, and many other factors. I say this to lay the foundation for understanding why we love the way we do and where our decisions come from if left to their natural inclinations. So part of any learning and growing process must contain the holding of new ideas before the mind. The mind can then determine what to hold onto as profitable or true and reject what isn't profitable, or false. We cannot grow in our relationships and understanding of how love works in its many forms if we don't find or experience new ideas about love and how it can and should manifest itself.

Any new idea must be based on a proved standard for it to be worth holding before the mind to be used in relationships or any decision-making process of what is true and good. I believe strongly that God and His ideas should be considered the standard for our ideas of love. First John 4:8 tells us that "God is Love" (KJV and most versions). He is the very essence of what love is and should be. So when we base our ideas of love on an understanding of how God loves and teaches us to share that love, in my opinion, is the most important idea to grasp in understanding how to enhance and maneuver through relationships of any kind.

I have witnessed long-time Christians and even pastors exhibit a lack of appropriate love all in the name of God, or their ideas of standing up for what they believe. All the while they left people hurt in their wake, in pursuit of being right. Let me give you a couple of examples from Gods word to show how He prioritizes these matters:

What Does Jesus Say?

Matthew 22:34–39 says, "Hearing that Jesus had silenced the Sadducees, the Pharisees got together. One of them, an expert in the law, tested him with this question: 'Teacher, which is the greatest commandment in the Law?' Jesus replied: "'Love the

Lord your God with all your heart and with all your soul and with all your mind." This is the first and greatest commandment. And the second is like it: "Love your neighbor as yourself.""

Several verses indicate this idea of loving God and others. And while many are familiar with these verses of scripture and can even quote them, not many know the following verse 40. "All the Law and the Prophets hang on these two commandments." This verse identifies the priority these verses have over all other teachings or commandments. All principles the law was meant to teach, and every idea the prophets were trying to convey, has been given context in which to operate. First Corinthians 13 further validates this point.

> If I speak in the tongues of men or of angels, but do not have love, I am only a resounding gong or a clanging cymbal. If I have the gift of prophecy and can fathom all mysteries and all knowledge, and if I have a faith that can move mountains, but do not have love, I am nothing. If I give all I possess to the poor and give over my body to hardship that I may boast, but do not have love, I gain nothing.
>
> Love is patient, love is kind. It does not envy, it does not boast, it is not proud. It does not dishonor others, it is not self-seeking, it is not easily angered, it keeps no record of wrongs. Love does not delight in evil but rejoices with the truth. It always protects, always trusts, always hopes, always perseveres.
>
> Love never fails. But where there are prophecies, they will cease; where there are tongues, they will be stilled; where there is knowledge, it will pass away. For we know in part and we prophesy in part, but when completeness

comes, what is in part disappears. When I was a child, I talked like a child, I thought like a child, I reasoned like a child. When I became a man, I put the ways of childhood behind me. For now we see only a reflection as in a mirror; then we shall see face to face. Now I know in part; then I shall know fully, even as I am fully known.

And now these three remain: faith, hope and love. But the greatest of these is love.

First, it is essential to note that every instance of love in this chapter is a translation of the word *agape*, the love of the mind and will, as God taught, not the love of the emotions, phileo. Since "God is Love" (1 John 4:8), we could take all instances of the word *love* in these verses and replace them with "God," and the passage would give us a remarkable picture of who God is. Can we do that with our names inserted?

I believe this chapter is very clear that in whatever knowledge you think you have, whatever understanding you have gained, or whatever acts on behalf of God or righteousness you exhibit, you must operate within the context of how they are done in love—more precisely, agape love. Anything less is an indication of our Christian maturity or understanding. Paul compared his use of knowledge and actions in the context of love to the difference in how he used ideas and reasoning between when he was a child and when he was a man. An apparent reference to his maturing in the use of gaining and using proper ideas of how to love. So without a growing understanding of how God defines agape love, there is little chance of adequately sharing God's precepts with those who need them. Nor would they want to hear them.

The first part of 1 John 4:8 says, "Whoever does not love does not know God." Again, this verse is using agape love. This bold statement indicates that the more we come to know and experience God, the more we will know how to love appropriately in the many experiences life will offer.

Loving Appropriately

Will we use love appropriately or inappropriately? I use the word *appropriately* because the word *unconditionally* doesn't always feel right. As we will see later, there are times when loving appropriately looks and feels very corrective or comes with boundaries, which may not feel unconditional. If we aren't learning more how to love appropriately, gaining new ideas about how God would have us love in any situation, then we aren't learning to know God better, and much of our understanding will be used in unloving ways. Put quite simply, this kind of love looks like this: "If I speak in the tongues of men or of angels, but do not have love, I am only a resounding gong or a clanging cymbal. If I have the gift of prophecy and can fathom all mysteries and all knowledge, and if I have a faith that can move mountains, but do not have love, I am nothing. If I give all I possess to the poor and give over my body to hardship that I may boast, but do not have love, I gain nothing" (1 Corinthians 13:1–3).

Then our maturity, if not based on a growing relationship with Jesus Christ and an understanding of how to love appropriately, will be based only on gaining knowledge without the wisdom to use it properly and it will be used for self-supporting reasons of all kinds. These would take intense therapy sessions to see and understand, and in the meantime, they would be very harmful to others and would inappropriately represent Jesus Christ to each other and a world that needs Him so desperately.

Which Team Are You On?

John 13:35 says, "By this everyone will know that you are my disciples, if you love one another." Just as there are obvious

11

ways to tell which football team I belong to (colors, uniforms, methodologies, and so forth), there is a definitive way to identify a true disciple of Jesus Christ: how he or she loves. For those disciples who don't yet know how to love like Jesus, let me say that others will question which team they are on. So we should keep seeking to learn how to exhibit what definitively identifies us as disciples of Christ.

Jesus had some very poignant and even controversial ideas about this love in Luke 6:27–38:

> But to you who are listening I say: love your enemies, do good to those who hate you, bless those who curse you, pray for those who mistreat you. If someone slaps you on one cheek, turn to them the other also. If someone takes your coat, do not withhold your shirt from them. Give to everyone who asks you, and if anyone takes what belongs to you, do not demand it back. Do to others as you would have them do to you.
>
> If you love those who love you, what credit is that to you? Even sinners love those who love them. And if you do good to those who are good to you, what credit is that to you? Even sinners do that. And if you lend to those from whom you expect repayment, what credit is that to you? Even sinners lend to sinners, expecting to be repaid in full. But love your enemies, do good to them, and lend to them without expecting to get anything back. Then your reward will be great, and you will be children of the Most High, because he is kind to the ungrateful and wicked. Be merciful, just as your Father is merciful.
>
> Do not judge, and you will not be judged. Do not condemn, and you will not be condemned.

Forgive, and you will be forgiven. Give, and it will be given to you. A good measure, pressed down, shaken together and running over, will be poured into your lap. For with the measure you use, it will be measured to you.

Then He added this: "Can the blind lead the blind? Will they not both fall into a pit? The student is not above the teacher, but everyone who is fully trained will be like their teacher" (Luke 6:39–40).

Living Testimonies

Is it a fair statement to say that any deviation from showing love in these ways is a testimony to how much we still need to learn to love the way Jesus did? And why is it so hard for some to accept this Lord we talk about when we misrepresent Him by the way we live?

Many say this kind of agape love is how Christians should love other Christians and that they will know Christians by how they love each other. Then this verse would need to be explained in this context: Luke 6:32–33 says, "If you love those who love you, what credit is that to you? Even sinners love those who love them. And if you do good to those who are good to you, what credit is that to you? Even sinners do that."

The Pharisees loved one another. They didn't, however, love those who disagreed with them. I know and have experienced pastors and Christians who don't show love for those who disagree with them. There is an old saying most Christians have heard, and is so relevant to this kind of love and being a true witness of the nature of the love Jesus represents. "People don't care how much you know until they know how much you care." Many well-meaning disciples of Christ know this saying, yet they forget its meaning when dealing with those they are trying to convince of their beliefs. Remember, people won't always remember what you said, but they will remember how you made them feel.

If I asked what the opposite of love is, most would respond with hate. Here is a new idea for that concept. If agape love is the idea of making a willful choice for the good of others, then the opposite would be not making a willful choice for the good of others or making a willful choice for the good of self. And you certainly don't need to hate someone to do that.

I think the bar just got raised.

CHAPTER 3

Why Agape and Phileo Love?

W hy do you suppose God gave us these ideas of agape and phileo love? I certainly can't speak for God, but I will try to offer my ideas on why God not only gave them to us but also wants us to understand them.

When we looked at the meaning of these two words in chapter one, we saw how the basic meanings show us that God wants us to understand the difference between phileo, a love of the heart or emotions, and agape, a love of the mind or will to choose good for others.

Why did God place in us the ability to have emotions? Now I don't pretend to offer an in-depth answer to this question, but I present a general understanding of why I believe we have been given emotions. As we have seen in chapter two, Jesus gave us the context in which to place everything we are to learn from the law and the prophets. He summed it all up in Matthew 22:38–40. "Love the Lord your God with all your heart and with all your soul and with all your mind. This is the first and greatest commandment. And the second is like it: Love your neighbor as yourself. All the Law and the Prophets hang on these two commandments."

In other words, everything is about relationships. So if everything is about relationships, wouldn't it make sense that

God would create us with what we needed to tend to those relationships the way He has designed them? And if everything is about relationships, wouldn't the greatest commandments in the law contain some valuable ideas about how to go about these relationships in a way that exemplifies the very essence of who God is—namely, love? I believe so. If this is all true, then I believe the reason He gave us emotions is to protect and nurture relationships. It's not hard to see this idea when it comes to having feelings of warmth or tenderness toward others, an easy concept to grasp how emotions help to nurture relationships. But what about anger?

Anger

At first glance, anger seems to have quite the opposite effect. But when we ponder the original idea of what anger is and how it should be used to nurture and protect relationships, we can see how it can accomplish this idea of nurturing and protecting. If someone is trying to hurt someone I love physically, wouldn't it be protective to allow my anger to intervene in a way that says to the offender, "You aren't in a proper relationship with those around you, and you won't be allowed to act this way"? Even if someone were trying to harm me physically, is it not appropriate for some form of anger to assist me in protecting myself? After all, "loving others as myself" indicates there is an appropriate way to love others and myself, and protection of these relationships from those who would violate relational boundaries seems appropriate.

Even Jesus Got Angry

In John 2, Jesus drove the money changers out of the temple. He seemed to be very angry when this event happened. He saw that these people were so far out of a right relationship with

His Father that it kindled anger in Him that prompted Him to nurture and protect a right relationship with the Father. We call this "righteous indignation," anger used for the right purpose of nurturing and protecting right relationships, not just as a means of consequences as so many see it.

Ephesians 4:26 (KJV) says, "Be angry and sin not." meaning, "Do not miss the mark in your relationships when you are provoked to anger." There is an appropriate anger God gave to nurture and protect relationships. Only a close look in the mirror God holds up to us can help us see the difference.

Fear

How about fear, an emotion no one likes to feel? Appropriate, God-given fear should drive us to act in relational ways. God often uses fear-based ideas to help us understand the consequences of separation from Him, not for the sole purpose of making us afraid but to let that fear guide us back into a proper relationship with Him. Fear can also trigger in us the fight-or-flight syndrome, which is meant to protect those around us and ourselves. If a lion found its way into my house while I was watching a movie with my family (obviously *The Lion King*), this situation would induce a fear-based response to attack it or get my family away from it. While not all fear-based responses are legitimate in nurturing or protecting relationships, this one seems to be a valid reason to be motivated by fear.

Anxiety

Anxiety is meant to cause uneasy feelings when relationships are out of order. Our souls have learned to use anxiety to get their needs met. Anyone who has fasted from something and is keenly aware of the body's responses can tell you that he or she goes through a period of anxiety, one that can be felt in the heart as the body secretes certain chemicals to let us know its cravings aren't being met. These chemicals can be felt in the heart at times and be mistaken for heart issues when it's the feeling of the body as it responds to not getting what it wants.

I fasted from coffee once, and being a daily drinker at the time; I thought I was having a slight heart attack because I felt a slight ache in my heart. Thankfully I recalled this feeling when I was on a three-day fast from food; I just waited it out, and the feeling went away when the soul realized it wasn't getting the coffee, and the body adjusted to not having the caffeine, and I found a peace from God that took its place. Now please understand that when we get the body addicted to something, it can be dangerous to try to fast from it, since the body can respond in drastic, unhealthy ways. I say these things to say that we can get our bodies used to some unhealthy habits, which aren't loving ourselves appropriately. One of the red flags is the anxiety our bodies create when they don't get whatever it is we have gotten them used to. Anxiety, when meant to nurture and protect relationships, works well when an important relationship in our lives isn't healthy or has been violated. These are what anxiety was intended for; not for selfish reasons when the soul doesn't get what it wants or is fearful of losing what it has.

Grief

Those who have lost a close loved one can testify to the literal pain in the heart as they grieve their loss. While none of us would want to experience this feeling, it is an indication of the importance of relationships in our lives. How I wish I could learn to love God so much that my heart would ache from being separated from Him. I have experienced this feeling at times but probably not nearly enough.

Grief and sadness are natural responses to broken relationships, whether broken from the intent of another to emotionally harm or something out of our control such as the loss of life. God places a high value on relationships, and when they are broken, there will undoubtedly be a triggering of other emotions as we feel the loss.

Happiness

True happiness comes from our relationships being in union the way God designed them, not just having what we think we want or need.

So where do emotions go wrong? It is when they are used for self-serving reasons which no longer are being used for the good of appropriate relationships with God, others, and ourselves.

Distorted Emotions

Anger has become one of the ways we use to try to manipulate others into relating in ways that meet our selfish needs and desires. When we take a God-given emotion designed to nurture and protect relationships and use it to protect our selfish agendas of meeting our own needs, we distort these gifts of emotions, which will always become detrimental to our relationships.

Our fears tend to be used to protect ourselves from things we are afraid may happen to us. Some people have been raised in an environment of abuse, which causes a legitimate reason to be fearful of others abusing them in the same way. This kind of self-protective fear keeps someone from enjoying healthy relationships. We can certainly understand why those with these hurts in their past have an automatic protective response to those around them. But these ideas placed in them were lies that told them how invaluable they were to relationships and that they somehow must protect themselves from any further abuse in their present, safe relationships. These people would benefit greatly from time spent with a Christian therapist to learn new ideas about who they really are, how lovable and valuable they are, and the kind of relationships they deserve to have because God says so. And they can learn to let new, truthful ideas push out old lies others placed in them.

Fear-based responses are the result of all sorts of lies unloving people have placed in us and circumstances we don't know how to process in healthy ways. Grief and sadness tell us the value of relationships. Having lost loved ones in my life, I cannot imagine the loss of such valuable relationships without having to go through the feelings that came with the loss. These can be difficult to work through for many since the pain can be deep and compounded by other losses. A sad reality we live with as we maneuver our way through a broken world. Thankfully, God has provided relief from all this pain with truth, hope, and His presence, both in this life and ultimately and permanently in the next.

Divorce brings great pain and grief. Having worked with several who experienced this pain, I have seen up close the results of breaking this relationship bond. The Bible describes divorce as the death of a marriage bond, and any death must be grieved for the loss experienced from it. It is always helpful to seek healing in other healthy relationships that will allow us to feel the pain of our loss and support us through it. Pastors, counselors, family, friends, and support groups will allow us safe places to express our grief while helping to take steps toward restoration.

As we can see from these very brief discussions about emotions, the idea of phileo is an operation of the heart. The heart feels deeply, protects intensely, and prompts strongly as it works its way through relationships of all kinds. And which of us is healthy enough to always be able to determine the motives of the heart to know whether what we are saying or doing is being done for the good of our relationships or out of a need to serve or protect our own needs and desires?

Therein lies the reason, in my mind, for a God-given form of love that makes choices based not solely on feelings, which may or may not prompt a selfish or unselfish response to whatever is happening. But will help us make decisions with more emphasis on a system of ideas designed to nurture and protect relationships and can be guided by precepts from God instead of worldly ideas and feelings that may or may not be healthy for making decisions. The heart is divided. There is a part of our heart that wants to love God with all our heart, soul, and mind; and to love others as ourselves. But there is a part of our heart that wants to serve ourselves. Even the most mature Christians must be honest about their humanity, and the sin that dwells in their members, understanding that they must always be aware of their hearts' weaknesses, lest they be tempted.

Agape love considers emotions but always tries to do what is best for all relationships concerned. Agape love isn't as natural as phileo since it is more of a learned system of processing and responding. And because it is learned, it can be taught new and better ways to make decisions. Jesus was the Master of agape love since He is "Emanuel," "God with Us." God is love, both agape, and phileo. He loves us with all His heart and will always do what is best for all concerned. Thus, the idea of learning agape and phileo. Learning to operate and guide our choices from both our hearts and our minds, from our feelings and idea systems of what is best for our relationships with God, others, and ourselves.

Godly Love (Agape and Phileo)

Look at these verses that show this truth in scripture. Both John 3:35 and 5:20 say, "The Father Loves the Son." A closer look reveals that 3:35 uses a form of agape, that the Father will always do what is best for His Son; while 5:20 uses a form of phileo, that He loves His Son with all His heart. So in our quest to conform to the image of His Son, I hope you can see the value of learning to distinguish and operate from both agape and phileo love.

21

CHAPTER 4

What's Your JQ?

A few years ago, I was going through a learning period and believed God wanted me to learn some new ideas. Because these new ideas were so distant from my life's experiences, I had a difficult time comprehending them, which was later apparent because circumstances caused me to feel so lost that I felt abandoned. St. John of the Cross, in a poem called "Dark Night of the Soul, "[2] wrote of his experiences in this place and of how God used it to refine him and bring him into a closer union with Himself.

My feeling of abandonment was my coming to the end of my resources to be able to deal with life in a way that would bring the well-being my soul sought after. Sometimes because God loves us so much, He takes us to this place where who we are at our core wouldn't allow us to go. Coming to the end of my resources left me feeling abandoned and alone with no answers to my souls' longings. This situation is sometimes also described as a "desert experience" or "wilderness experience," such as the one Moses experienced in the desert. Sometimes the only way we can see the new ideas God has for us is for Him to take us

---

[2] St. John of The Cross, *"Dark Night of The Soul,"* CCEL.org website and special contents copyright (1993-2015) Harry Plantinga

to the end of the ideas we have. I often say there are only two ways to increase our faith—to seek new ideas about God and let those ideas, when understood properly, increase our faith; or to be taken to the end of the faith we have so we can find and experience the new level of faith. Only God can know what is needed, and it is often measured out as a product of our seeking and wanting more.

My Dark Night

I found myself getting out of bed at about three o'clock one morning and standing in the shower, feeling lost, as the water tried to wash away the aloneness. My wife heard the water running at the odd hour, came in, and asked, "What are you doing?"

I merely said, "I don't know. Something is wrong, but I don't know what it is."

Have you ever felt like something was wrong or out of order, but there was nothing in your idea system or experience to deal with it? I now understand that this wilderness experience was God lovingly taking me to the end of myself so I could experience Him in a deeper way.

A Meeting in a Hotel Room

I later told my wife I was going to a hotel room to be alone with God. I know this may sound like a strange place, but I knew I needed more than just a couple of hours, so it seemed like a good place to go for an extended period without interruption.

So I checked in, placed the "Do Not Disturb" sign on the door and laid on the bed. No food, no phone. Just a Bible and a notepad. I said to God, "Here I am. I'm not leaving until You meet with me." This was with apprehension because the hotel wasn't letting me stay for free. So I lay there on that hotel bed for twenty-four hours as God began to teach me how to detach from the world. Sometimes it's only through this kind of detachment from the world that we can hear what He is trying to tell us.

I won't go into the details of this twenty-four-hour period here since it could probably be another book in itself. I will summarize the experience by sharing the lessons I learned.

1. It taught me how to disengage from the world long enough to be able to hear Him without all the noise. Building a home base for me to go to (and how to get there quicker) so I wouldn't need twenty-four hours to disengage and open up to Him.
2. It taught me the principles of being in His presence, learning how to try to live in that presence, and not having to disengage so much to find it. Because of this home base experience, I am learning to experience His presence more and more as I live out my experiences in this world, which I believe help me to be more open to His ideas and the principles behind the written word He has left us.

What Is JQ?

This discussion brings us to the title of this chapter, "What's Your JQ?" Most of us are familiar with the term *IQ*, which stands for "intelligence quotient." IQ is a measure of the intelligence we possess. I believe God taught me the principle of "JQ" or "Jesus Quotient" as a measure of the amount of His presence I possess or am aware of. And this is how I experience and explain it: From the time you wake up until the time you pillow your head at night, how much do you feel or are aware of the presence of Jesus Christ in your life? I use the scale of 0 to 100 percent to try to put some measure to it—0 meaning I never feel or am aware of His presence and 100 meaning I always feel or am aware of

His presence. Now, this number isn't good or bad, not right or wrong. It is just one's idea of how to measure the amount of time during their waking hours when they feel, or are aware of, the presence of God, Jesus Christ, and the Holy Spirit in their lives and daily experiences.

After explaining this concept, I began asking people what they believed their JQ was. I asked people I knew, including pastors. I even presented the idea to a congregation of about thirteen hundred one Sunday; I explained the concept and asked them to bow their heads and raise their hands. I asked who was between 0 and 10 percent, 10 and 20 percent, 20 and 30 percent, and so forth until I reached 90 and 100 percent.

I was astounded by the results. The vast majority fell between the 20 and 30 percent range. I was amazed because this response meant that most people didn't feel or experience His presence 70 to 80 percent of the time. I suppose I shouldn't have been surprised by this response since I knew that JQ number well in my own experience before God and my experience gave me new ideas about it. The problem is that if we don't feel or are aware of God's presence 70 to 80 percent of the time, we fight our sin temptations 70 to 80 percent of the time by ourselves or by our own thought processes and willpower, a recipe for inevitable failure. The classic hymn "I Need Thee Every Hour" offers this verse concerning this idea:

> I need Thee every hour,
> Stay Thou near by;
> Temptations lose their power
> When Thou art nigh

Walking with Us

I often ask this question: If Jesus Christ physically walked through the door right now and walked up to you, took your hand, and said, "I am going to walk with you the rest of your life and will always be right here, holding your hand," would this experience change the way you live? The way you act? The things you think about? The things you fear? For me, the thought of holding His hand and allowing myself to do or think some of the things I used to, isn't as easy anymore.

I have worked with men on managing their thought lives. In my office, I had a picture on the wall of Jesus Christ I received as a gift from my brother. I spoke to men about this JQ principle and about how easy it usually is to allow those errant thoughts in their minds. Then I held this picture of Jesus Christ in front of their faces and asked them to look into the eyes of this picture and try to have those thoughts. Without fail, everyone said he couldn't have those thoughts. Why? It was just a picture. But in their minds, it was a real and present idea of Jesus Christ, and they couldn't allow themselves to think such things while in His presence. This evidence shows the power of our minds to control our thoughts when we have the right reasons to do so. I also asked them whether, while walking through the mall and literally holding the hand of Jesus Christ, they would give in to the temptation to look in the window of a lingerie store. Well, guess what? If He said He would never leave us (Deuteronomy 31:8; Hebrews 13:15), He is standing right there with every thought we have or every action we allow. The only difference is our not feeling or being aware of His presence. Or maybe even purposely ignoring it.

I asked them, and ask myself today, what do we do with the presence of Jesus Christ when we give in to such things, even when we allow unhealthy or unloving thoughts? As I practice His presence more and more, I find it harder and harder to give in to my temptations. Oh, how I wish I could get my JQ up to 100 percent. But I know that in my human nature, I have so much in me that is self-seeking, that 100 percent seems impossible. But what I have experienced is that, while I used to struggle with temptations 70 to 80 percent of the time because I lacked awareness of His presence, my experience has turned into struggling much less because of believing in and being aware of His presence. I cannot allow the things I used to because of this increased practice of recognizing His presence, and I'm not afraid of the same things I used to fear. Practicing the presence of Jesus Christ in my daily life and routines have changed the way I act and think throughout each day. Now, this statement isn't a claim that my human desires never win; it just means the struggle is reduced because of this practice. And the nice thing is that I'm not trying to follow some law or rule to do so, but I'm trying not to sin (miss the mark) against the one I love. And learning to love God back for what He has done for me and taught me translates into learning to love those around me and even myself in more healthy and appropriate ways.

I want to be very clear here; this isn't all because of my own efforts. It would be counterproductive if I thought I could achieve a better awareness or sense Christ's presence more all because I tried harder. This issue is more about submission than trying harder. As I study God's word and repent (change my mind) about His ideas compared to mine, I can then buy into His ideas and submit to them because I believe them to be good and right.

Selling Old Ideas and Buying New Ones

Check out the ideas in this lesson from Jesus in Matthew 13:44–46: "The kingdom of heaven is like treasure hidden in a field. When a man found it, he hid it again, and then in his joy went and sold all he had and bought that field. Again, the kingdom of heaven is like a merchant looking for fine pearls. When he found one of great value, he went away and sold everything he had and bought it."

The ideas here can be summed up in seeing the value of

something I have found compared to what I have. We all have an idea system, a way of thinking and processing that is who we are and who we have learned to be. When we learn about new ideas and ways of thinking that come from God, we hold them up to each other in the mind's eye and compare their value to us. When we change our minds in seeing that God's ideas are more valuable than ours (repentance), we sell out our old ideas and buy, or hold on to, the new ones. This is all done as a process of the Holy Spirit finding new and creative ways to present these new ideas to us. While I believe we have a choice in what we do with these new ideas, the Holy Spirit is hard at work presenting them in new and different ways to help us see what is true. The Greek word *truth* (*Alethea*), literally interpreted, means "not hidden." If something is false, the accurate ideas are being hidden from our understanding. When the Holy Spirit holds up ideas before our minds, we evaluate them for the value they bring to us. This is why, when our minds and hearts are turned inward, we evaluate His ideas based on how they will satisfy our desires, and we often reject them in the beginning. Sometimes this requires bringing us to the end of our resources, our ideas about how to best meet our needs. Then we may be willing to hold His ideas up to the light, where they will no longer be hidden from our understanding, repent, receive forgiveness, and begin learning how to apply the new ideas to our relationships with God, others, and ourselves.

The Holy Spirit Is Our Helper

Always remember that the Holy Spirit was sent to us to allow us to experience the presence of God and Jesus in our everyday lives. John 14:16–17 says this truth this way: "And I will ask the Father, and he will give you another advocate to help you and be with you forever—the Spirit of truth. The world cannot accept him, because it neither sees him nor knows him. But you know him, for he lives with you and will be in you." John 16:7 says, "But very truly I tell you, it is for your good that I am going away. Unless I go away, the Advocate will not come to you; but if I go, I will send him to you." The "Advocate" spoken of here is a translation of the Greek word *paraklete*, more literally, one who comes alongside and shouts for us. Thank You, Holy Spirit, for always being by our sides and shouting to the Father on our behalf. If only we knew how to live as if You were there all the time; because You are.

I love to talk about the "wilderness experience" or "Dark Night of The Soul," since many can relate to these ideas. I speak of that twenty-four-hour period of learning to try to help them understand why God may allow us to feel some of these feelings of abandonment and aloneness, and how I began to practice this presence, which He taught me was available. Jesus makes some remarkable statements to validate these ideas in Hebrews 13:5: "Never will I leave you; never will I forsake you." Matthew 28:20 says, "And surely I am with you always, to the very end of the age."

Using Reason

Reason told me that if Jesus Christ said to me He would never leave me and was with me always, then the only reason I wasn't experiencing His presence was that I didn't feel it or wasn't aware of it. I use both ideas of feeling and being aware because, in my human emotions, my feelings come and go. It's nice to feel His presence, but when I don't feel it, I'm learning to be conscious of it because nothing has changed. What a glorious revelation this was as I learned to start practicing this presence.

One way was to acknowledge His presence with me as I was walking through the local mall. I would walk with my right hand clenched as if I were holding His hand simply to remind me that He was right there with me every moment. And even if I didn't feel it, I could be aware of it. This concept also helped me to understand the principle of my sin always being in His presence, and 70 to 80 percent of the time, I could sin as if He wasn't there. My new ideas of not just following commandments, because they were the law, and following because I wanted to love Him in return now took on a whole new meaning. It wasn't so easy to sin when I was aware of His presence. This change soon began to affect what I allowed myself to view on TV, on the computer, or even what I allowed my eyes or thoughts to be fixed on. The difference between feeling and being aware of His presence relates very closely to the ideas of phileo and agape love, of feelings and mindfulness. Here are some more verses that speak to this idea of God being with us.

Promises of His Presence from Scripture

The virgin will conceive and give birth to a son, and they will call him Immanuel [which means "God with us"]. (Matthew 1:23)

Have I not commanded you? Be strong and courageous. Do not be afraid; do not be discouraged, for the Lord your God will be with you wherever you go. (Joshua 1:9)

For I am convinced that neither death nor life, neither angels nor demons, neither the present nor the future, nor any powers, neither height nor depth, nor anything else in all creation, will be able to separate us from the Love of God that is in Christ Jesus our Lord. (Romans 8:38–39)

And I will ask the Father, and he will give you another advocate to help you and be with you forever—the Spirit of truth. The world cannot accept him, because it neither sees him nor knows him. But you know him, for he lives with you and will be in you. (John 14:16–17)

Where can I go from your Spirit?
Where can I flee from your presence?
If I go up to the heavens, you are there;
if I make my bed in the depths, you are there.
If I rise on the wings of the dawn,
if I settle on the far side of the sea,
even there your hand will guide me,
your right hand will hold me fast.
(Psalm 139:7–10)

"Am I only a God nearby," declares the Lord, "and not a God far away? Who can hide in secret places so that I cannot see them?" declares the Lord. "Do not I fill heaven and earth?" (Jeremiah 23:23–24)

"The Lord himself goes before you and will be with you; he will never leave you nor forsake you. Do not be afraid; do not be discouraged." (Deuteronomy 31:8)

The Lord is my shepherd, I lack nothing.
He makes me lie down in green pastures,
he leads me beside quiet waters,
he refreshes my soul.
He guides me along the right paths
for his name's sake.
Even though I walk
through the darkest valley,

I will fear no evil,
for you are with me;
your rod and your staff,
they comfort me.
You prepare a table before me
in the presence of my enemies.
You anoint my head with oil;
my cup overflows.
Surely your goodness and Love will follow me
all the days of my life,
and I will dwell in the house of the Lord
forever.
(Psalm 23)

He is always "with us."

What's your JQ?

I'm learning the depths of His love and presence, which also reveal the depths of my sin.

CHAPTER 5

What Is Sin?

Learning the depth of God's love and presence has also revealed the extent of my sin. First, I would like to lay a foundation for this chapter, that foundation being the total forgiveness of our sins when we acknowledge who Jesus Christ is and what He has done for us. Many good books lay out the ideas of repentance and faith in a way that helps us to understand the depth of what Jesus Christ has done for us. That all our sins—past, present, and future—are forgiven because of His taking our place and providing a way for us not to have to suffer the consequences of that sin. The Bible is the standard, and any book written as an explanation must be to promote a further understanding of what the Bible is trying to convey. That is no different from this book being a personal explanation of my understanding of what God, through the Bible, is trying to teach us about love.

Let me say that if you haven't accepted this free gift of unconditional love and forgiveness, this relationship really does begin with just a simple acknowledgment of who Jesus is and what He has done for us. You can stop and accept this gift right now by similarly communicating with God as this prayer to Him:

> Dear Father, I believe that Jesus Christ is Your Son and that He loved me so much that He gave His life for me to provide a way for me to spend eternity with You in heaven. In the best way that I know how today, I want to learn to love You and Him back in a way that honors You and helps me to love others and myself in more healthy and appropriate ways. I receive and thank You for Your forgiveness, and I ask You, Holy Spirit, to teach me how to love God, others, and myself better.

The reason I need to lay this foundation, is that I am about to reveal what I believe is a deeper understanding of the depth of sin than most people have ever heard before. This more in-depth understanding of sin should bring with it a deeper understanding of what Jesus Christ has done for us and should cause us to want to love Him back. It isn't meant to lay guilt or shame on any believer that doesn't belong to them, because he or she has received forgiveness already.

I wholeheartedly believe that the Bible (especially the New Testament) isn't meant to be translated into rules to follow but to teach us how to love God, others, and ourselves; and it shows us what this looks like when we believers don't do it well. The Bible is a book of principles and ideas about proper relationships, first with God and from those ideas how to be in a proper relationship with each other and even ourselves. We all need new ideas from God about how to do this. When we make the relationship rules to follow, we miss the relational lessons and turn it into a one-two-three guide to try to avoid the consequences of our sin, having little or no value for proper relationships with anyone, and we certainly don't in ourselves have the ability to follow any rule system closely enough to satisfy its standards. So hang on as I hope to help you see the depth of our sin.

The Depth of Sin

The English word *sin* comes from the Greek word *hamartia*. This word, literally translated, means "not hitting the mark" or "missing the mark." (Trust me, I am staying out of the weeds to explain this one.) So what is the mark? Most have played some kind of game similar to darts, in which the object of scoring is to throw something at a target. The target would contain the highest score area in the center, referred to as the bull's-eye, and then areas around it that would be considered progressively lower scores in concentric circles around the bull's-eye, becoming lower the farther away the target is hit. The center or bull's-eye would be considered the mark. Anything outside this center area would be considered missing the mark and would be given less or no value. What is the mark in our faith? So glad you asked. In the Old Testament, from the very onset of communication with Adam, God made the first simple mark very clear in Genesis 2:16–17. "And the Lord God commanded the man, 'You are free to eat from any tree in the garden; but you must not eat from the tree of the knowledge of good and evil, for when you eat from it you will certainly die.'"

Many see this verse as God laying the first law and what the punishment would be if that law were to be violated. I understand this verse a bit differently. I believe God loved Adam, and the warning came as an act of this love. That death (literally, separation)—both the separation of the body from the soul and the separation of the soul from God—was something God didn't want Adam to have to experience. God warned him that the consequence of not loving Him back would separate him in devastating ways. And all subsequent laws were ways to protect man from experiencing any further separation from Him and each other.

I don't personally believe God's first interaction with man was to give him life, set him in the garden, and give him a temptation that, if he gave into it, would carry with it an enormous punishment. I truly believe He loved Adam and wanted Adam to know what wasn't good for his relationship with Himself. He offered Adam an opportunity to love Him back by honoring the way He loved Adam. The very next verse exemplifies this love for Adam. "The Lord God said, 'It is not good for the man to be alone. I will make a helper suitable for him'" (Genesis 2:18).

I believe that, in that first relationship between God and man, God wanted to be the one to meet all of Adam's basic human needs. He wanted to be his everything. But God recognized that in Adam's (and subsequently our) unloving disobedience or lack of returning His love, Adam didn't know how to let God be his everything and allow Him to meet all his basic human needs, so he tried to meet some of them himself. God responded, not with anger or with punishment (although Adam still had to experience the consequences of his choice, death—separation of the spirit from the body, physical death, and separation of the soul or spirit from God, spiritual death) but with love by saying, "It is not good for man to be alone."

What? First, Adam wasn't alone. God was right there with him. But Adam didn't know how to let God be his all in all. God responded by giving him a "helper," literally someone who was the opposite of him to help him. What an incredible act of love when He was about to be jilted by the one He was showing such an amazing display of love. It was kind of like God saying that He knew Adam didn't know how to let Him be enough, and He gave him someone to make up the difference until He would restore him and bring him to live with Him forever.

Further evidence for this is in the New Testament idea given in Matthew 22:30. "At the resurrection, people will neither marry nor be given in marriage." In heaven, this relationship with the helper won't be necessary in the same way because Adam (and all of us) will experience how God can meet all his (and our) needs.

The Old Testament went on to lay down all kinds of laws, rules, and consequences because of man's inability and lack of desire to love Him back. The Old Testament covenant was based on a system of laws because of man's desire not to love God in return. People's hearts were turned toward themselves, and they thought they could be good enough to satisfy any system of rules. This whole system was, in my mind, set in motion to show us how inwardly focused we were; if we thought we could be good enough to be in union with the Father, then here were the rules to follow to achieve this. However, the system turned out to be a giant mirror for us to see that we could never be good enough to meet the requirements of this law. And it set the stage for an understanding of God's coming sacrifice of His Son to fulfill this law on our behalf. Now I said to fulfill these requirements, not to do away with them.

So in the New Testament age, the legal requirements of the law to have union with the Father, have been satisfied. Those who have repented (literally "changed their minds") about thinking they could be good enough, can now receive the gift of union with the Father through this change of thinking and accept this gift that is freely offered. If an understanding of what God has done for us in this capacity isn't enough to turn our hearts toward Him, then there is more work that needs to be done to allow people to come to the end of their own resources before they see the value of this gift. Many don't understand the value because they still have false ideas that they can do life just fine on their own, and they aren't convinced that the next age holds good or bad consequences based on what they did with this knowledge in this age. I do believe His love pursues us in incredibly persuasive ways to try to change our minds about the Father, Son, Holy Spirit, life, death, love, forgiveness, and so forth … all for our good.

Now I know there are those who will stand on the idea of God being righteous and holy, and this is true. The law was laid down for man to honor that, and they are right if we were still under the Old Testament covenant. But why would God lay down a standard that couldn't be met and punish people when they didn't meet it after He had fulfilled the requirements of the law? I believe that when we understand that He is righteous and holy (because He is) and still offered this extravagant love to us, this knowledge should cause us to want to love Him back. He has our best good at heart and wants us to love Him in return by honoring what He says is best and good for us. And this is loving Him back. Man just wasn't able to get all that, so He displayed His great love for us by sending His one and only Son, Jesus Christ, to receive in Himself the consequences of man not loving God back. If God was so bent on making man follow His righteous and holy standards, why did He continually provide ways back to Himself when man couldn't and wouldn't conform? If someone wants to stand on trying to follow the righteous and holy standards of God, then I offer these New Testament ideas:

> For all who rely on the works of the law are under a curse, as it is written: "Cursed is everyone who does not continue to do everything written in the Book of the Law." Clearly no one who relies on the law is justified before God, because "the righteous will live by faith. (Galatians 3:10–11)

> For whoever keeps the whole law and yet stumbles at just one point is guilty of breaking all of it. (James 2:10)

The main point is that I have never met one person who said he or she believed in Jesus to avoid going to hell, who didn't need to learn about how much God desperately loved him or her to try to overcome the fear placed in him or her. Jesus did talk about hell, but it wasn't even close to His primary message of evangelism (sharing the good news). His primary message by far was the idea of the Kingdom of Heaven on earth and what is available to us here and now in this age and the next. We need to be careful about using hell to promote obedience since we aren't saved because of our obedience but because of trust in who Jesus is and what He has done for us. I understand that for some, the unbelieving or immature, they may need to hear this kind of message to consider the consequences of their choices, and hell may be used to try to get them to think about the direction they are going. But they will also need to learn and mature into loving God and others for the right reasons, not just to avoid hell.

For most people I have been around, especially in the current culture, they are more willing to respond to a message of love than one of judgment and condemnation. I will start with this message of love for young and old alike, and if they cannot or won't respond in kind, then the only alternative is to try to make them afraid of the consequences. It doesn't take much love to try to condemn others because they don't believe the way I do. I have seen Christians throw the idea of hell around as if they could care less who may have to endure it, but it sure made them feel righteous to do so. Besides, any unbeliever can see the logs in our eyes, even if we want to act like they aren't there. But when we offer the truth in love, others may listen, meaning they must believe we are talking to them because we care about them, not just because we have been taught we are right and need to shove it down their throats and somehow elevate ourselves when we point out the faults of others. Teaching in love and not practicing condemnation (except as a last truth-in-love resort) are acts of love that can come only with continual growth as we learn to be more like Jesus.

We are separated from our God because we have all missed the mark. The only thing that brings life or union with the Father is accepting His gift of Jesus Christ, not changing behavior, following the rules, trying to avoid hell, or outperforming our wrong choices with right ones. These things should happen because we grow in our understanding of how much God loves us and has proved that love, and we begin to learn to love Him in return. Avoiding the consequence of hell will never teach us how to love God, others, or ourselves appropriately, which is the context of all knowledge and teaching unless it is offered in the context of what God through Jesus Christ has done for us. Yes, hell is real, and everyone should understand what Jesus Christ has saved us from. And it should be taught so we can understand what it is and be ready to answer questions if asked about what we believe about hell. But avoiding hell isn't the premise of our faith; learning to love God in return is, and from learning how He loves, we learn to love others and ourselves appropriately. And that is the context for everything contained in our faith and the new covenant.

My experience in trying to help people learn to love appropriately tells me that people change, fundamentally speaking, for one of two reasons.

1. Because they understand that their choices and behavior aren't loving God, others, or themselves appropriately, and they want to make changes to do so.
2. Or because they are no longer willing to pay the price for what their choices are costing them.

Unfortunately, most fall into category number two. But consequence avoidance isn't what God had in mind, although I'm sure He understands this is how we often operate and sometimes uses it to get us moving in the right direction or what I would term as moving from immaturity to maturity. And in the new covenant, we aren't in danger of the consequences just because we have missed the mark; we are all guilty of that. The only reason a person would experience any separation from the Father is how he or she responded to the knowledge he or she was given about Jesus Christ. Jesus hit all the marks for us, and we are all given different amounts of knowledge and ideas about Him.

Don't Play in the Street

A human example would be how we teach our children not to play in the street. When our children are small, they want to walk where they want. When they go to step in the street, we stop them and tell them no. If they continue to try to walk into the street, we may progress to a swat to help them understand that we won't allow them to do so. In their immaturity, they don't understand the consequences of their actions. We don't spend much time explaining the consequences of what a large car will do to a small human body. They wouldn't comprehend our explanation. So we use a measured consequence to help avoid a larger consequence, done out of love and for what is best for our child. If we lose our temper, we have now crossed the line into consequences to manipulate behavior for our own well-being, which isn't loving (more about that later).

However, you don't want to spank your eighteen-year-olds for going out in the street, so at some point, you begin to teach them why they shouldn't play in the street. Then someday they won't play in the street for the right reason, not just to avoid getting spanked. They won't play in the street because it is unsafe, and loving themselves properly, also means keeping themselves safe and avoiding causing harm to others.

Maturing

As we mature, we learn to minimize the risks we took when we were younger because we now have families we need to think about, and at some point in our idea system about being used by God, keeping ourselves healthy and usable should become part of our thinking. I believe the whole idea of hell sometimes is used with the same thought as the street theory. If we try to scare others into avoiding the consequences, maybe they won't do what they do. The difference is, not doing certain things or trying not to sin or trying not to miss the mark won't keep us out of hell. The consequence of an afterlife in hell is based on sin or missing the mark, and it takes only one miss to be guilty. We have no power in ourselves to live perfectly, so we are all found guilty. It is only through accepting God's gift of love in Jesus Christ that we avoid the consequences of our afterlife choices and begin learning how to love properly. I don't honestly believe that avoiding hell is the primary reason God wants you to know and accept His Son. In John 10:10, He says, "I have come that they may have life."

Remember that death means separation, and life means union. He came that we would have union with the Father. Yes, we should know what it is we are being saved from by the death of Jesus, but if consequence avoidance is the only reason we say we believe, are we truly in union with the Father? Isn't consequence avoidance just more selfishness? And why do we use the very thing we are trying to get people not to be to motivate them: selfishness? If everything the law and the prophets had to teach us, hang on the two statements of loving God and loving others as ourselves, then doesn't this same principle apply when it teaches about salvation? Everything must always be in the context of appropriate love. Now I realize that if we determine that someone is either incapable of understanding or simply rebellious and doesn't want to understand, that proper love would be to warn of the consequences and possibly use a measured response to help him, or her see the truth. But why do so many begin there when they are speaking to those who are able to understand and may receive it if presented in a loving context?

I pray that as I learn to be more like Christ, to think and live and feel more like Him, that this kind of love is more of a natural outflow of who I am becoming than a measure of trying hard to do the right things. There is absolutely nothing wrong with the old WWJD (What Would Jesus Do?) symbol. But I failed at trying to do any right things so many times and hurt so many people that I hope to be more like Him, and in living in His presence (JQ), becoming more like Him, I naturally love more like He does. I realize this is a lifetime project, but God, others, and I are worth it.

I Apologize

At this point, I would like to stop and apologize from the depth of my soul to anyone I have ever made to feel in an unloving way. I suppose we would all have circumstances and people in our past that, in a more mature moment, we would change or apologize to. It isn't always wise to go back and apologize when someone has moved on or is in other relationships, but if possible and if it causes no further harm, apologies can help others to know that something was done unintentionally or out of immaturity and selfishness that didn't know how to prevent it and we have learned how we hurt them and are remorseful for doing so. I certainly don't have the wisdom always to know when to try to make amends for past hurts, and I pray that God will guide us in areas where amends may be in order.

We Christians need to learn how to explain how the actions and thoughts of others aren't loving God, others, or ourselves appropriately, not just trying to point to a law to judge and condemn them as if following the law could save them. The problem with our not understanding the relational principles of appropriate love contained within the principles of the law is that we can give no real reason except to say that God calls it sin, and so do we. God is just saying that He wants us to see how much we are missing the mark in all our relationships and how much we need His Son, so we don't have to pay the price for it. Then we learn how to love like He does, to "hit the mark."

Keeping Score?

We could never quantify the amount of missing the marks we have in showing appropriate love in all our relationships, beginning with God, then others, and then ourselves. This tally would most certainly be exponentially higher than any count of the times we broke a rule or law. This view of "missing the mark" (sin) is much bigger than most of us have ever been taught, and it certainly should put what Jesus has done for us on a much grander scale. If that doesn't prompt at least a desire to return that love (obedience), then the following verse may need to be applied: "Furthermore, just as they did not think it worthwhile to retain the knowledge of God, so God gave them over to a depraved mind, so that they do what ought not to be done" (Romans 1:28).

The word *depraved* is also sometimes translated as "reprobate." The Greek word is *adokimos*. It is the kind of mind that can no longer pass the test because it cannot even distinguish the difference between right and wrong. I believe it's a mind that cannot distinguish between loving and unloving thoughts or actions, or lacking the desire to do so. First Corinthians 5:5 says, "Hand this man over to Satan for the destruction of the flesh, so that his spirit may be saved on the day of the Lord." This is when God pulls His hands back from these people so they might see the unloving nature and consequences of their actions and repent (change their minds). We can honor God for His justice and righteousness, so we don't need to suffer the consequences, or we can honor His justice and righteousness because we are learning to love Him. Which would you want if you were God?

Please remember these words when trying to help someone understand who God is and what He stands for. Second Timothy 2:24–26 (NASB) says: "The Lord's bond-servant must not be quarrelsome, but be kind to all, able to teach, patient when wronged, with gentleness correcting those who are in opposition, if perhaps God may grant them repentance leading to the knowledge of the truth, and they may come to their senses and escape from the snare of the devil, having been held captive by him to do his will."

First John 4:18 says, "There is no fear in love. But perfect love drives out fear, because fear has to do with punishment. The one who fears is not made perfect in love." Why would we try to place fear in someone when this is the very thing "perfect love" is trying to drive out?

While we are all born with a sin nature, we must remember that we don't wake up one morning possessed. We build a relationship with sin and temptation. Similar to when our children miss the mark in their relationship with us, we don't want them to hide from us, do we? We want them to come out from behind their little trees so we can help them see what they have done. To understand that there are consequences for certain unloving behaviors and how to better do the right, loving things moving forward, we need to get better at explaining why things are unloving and not just wrong.

CHAPTER 6

Being Conformed

Romans 8:29 says, "For those God foreknew he also predestined to be conformed to the image of his Son." What does this mean? I believe it means we learn and grow to think, feel, and respond more like Jesus Christ so what comes out of us isn't an effort to follow any rule system but a natural outflow of the people we are becoming at the core. So if the "mark" is thinking, feeling, and responding like Jesus Christ, then every time we don't, we "miss the mark." This doesn't mean we broke a rule. I would hate to think that my forgiveness is based on following all the rules correctly, and the Bible is very clear that if we try to do it this way, we had better follow them all perfectly, or we are guilty of all of them. James 2:1–11 says,

> My brothers and sisters, believers in our glorious
> Lord Jesus Christ must not show favoritism.
> Suppose a man comes into your meeting
> wearing a gold ring and fine clothes, and a poor
> man in filthy old clothes also comes in. If you
> show special attention to the man wearing fine
> clothes and say, "Here's a good seat for you," but
> say to the poor man, "You stand there" or "Sit on
> the floor by my feet," have you not discriminated

among yourselves and become judges with evil thoughts?

Listen, my dear brothers and sisters: Has not God chosen those who are poor in the eyes of the world to be rich in faith and to inherit the kingdom he promised those who love him? But you have dishonored the poor. Is it not the rich who are exploiting you? Are they not the ones who are dragging you into court? Are they not the ones who are blaspheming the noble name of him to whom you belong?

If you really keep the royal law found in Scripture, to "love your neighbor as yourself," you are doing right. But if you show favoritism, you sin and are convicted by the law as lawbreakers. For whoever keeps the whole law and yet stumbles at just one point is guilty of breaking all of it. For he who said, "You shall not commit adultery," also said, "You shall not murder." If you do not commit adultery but do commit murder, you have become a lawbreaker."

The Consequences

So what are the consequences of missing the mark? Romans 6:23 says, "For the wages of sin is death, but the gift of God is eternal life in Christ Jesus our Lord." (Death = Separation, Life = Union) The difference is when we miss the mark of God's perfect standard for love, Jesus Christ, there are no lesser scores to achieve. We either hit the mark, or we miss it.

Romans 3:23 tells us we have all missed the mark: "For all have sinned and fall short of the glory of God." When we understand that sin, missing the mark, is about our not loving like Jesus did and not just violating a rule, we begin to see that sin is so much bigger and more prevalent than any of us has ever imagined. And since Jesus Christ died on our behalf to cover these sins, this truth should start to give us a much bigger picture of what He has done for us, since our missing the mark in all our relationships is many and continual. If that fact doesn't stir a love and dependence, then we haven't looked directly into the mirrors God holds up to show us who we really are and where we are in relation to Him, others, and ourselves.

Picture Perfect

You see, this is what the Bible is all about—showing us a picture of perfect love and then holding a mirror up so we can see where we aren't living out the image of Jesus Christ, which the Father longs to conform us to. He is loving and compassionate in His quest to teach us how to love like Jesus because that is a win-win outcome for all. An equestrian mentor of mine, Clinton Anderson, has a quote that fits here when training horses. "Be as gentle as possible, but as firm as necessary." I believe God operates perfectly in this manner when He holds up these mirrors for us to learn how to love for our own good and the good of those around us.

The word *death* means "separation." Life is the opposite of death and means "union." So the consequence of sin, of missing the mark, is separation from God, both in this life and in the next. The natural consequences in this life would be broken relationships and/or legal consequences since human law is based on how we must live in proper relation to each other or face the consequences to try to correct our behavior. But accepting the gift means union with God both in this life and in the next. As we understand and learn from this union, conforming more to the image of Jesus, it changes the way we relate to each other in this life. In another chapter, I deal with the consequences of broken relationships in this world and how they play out from this relationship with God. Receiving this gift doesn't necessarily mean we won't need to face the penalty for what we have done to others in this life. But it can still change who we are and how we proceed through the rest of this life, and it allows others to learn from our mistakes.

Looking Closer at the Mark

Now, let's define the "mark" a little more clearly, putting together biblical ideas. If we say the mark is thinking, feeling, and responding like Jesus Christ, then what are we thinking, feeling, and responding to?

Earlier we showed that in Matthew 22:37–40, Jesus taught us that all that the law and prophets were trying to teach us was summed up in loving God and others as ourselves. If Christ is the "mark" or bull's-eye for this kind of love, then every time we "miss the mark," we deserve the consequence of separation both in this life and in the next. Thank God for providing a way not only to escape this consequence but also to give us union with Him and others in this life and the next. Remember that a proper relationship with God isn't just about, or even primarily about, escaping the consequences of missing the mark but more about a union with Him and others.

But now, having a better understanding of what sin or missing the mark is, please take the time to dwell on how many times you and I have missed the mark of loving God, others, and ourselves in appropriate, Christlike ways. This understanding of sin is so much bigger than the idea of breaking a few laws or rules—that every time I don't show appropriate love for God, others, or myself, I am guilty and deserve the consequences of separation. Again, the very basis of our system of law and retribution is to apply a measured consequence to restore the person to proper relationships with others. The idea of following rules becomes so much easier than trying to love like Jesus does in every relationship in our lives. But I believe that is the standard or mark. Thank God that He provides relief from these consequences and now offers us an opportunity to learn how to love like Jesus.

The School of Jesus

My mentor friend Paul Carlisle, whom I mentioned earlier, spoke in terms of being in the school of Jesus. Learning to think, feel, and respond more like He would. Not just trying to do what He did as a means of right behavior; but through thinking, feeling, and becoming more like Him, we respond more like Him because we are more like Him in our depths, and it is a lot easier to respond from who we are than to try to act a certain way. And God and others perceive this as a more genuine love than just trying to say or do the right thing as a matter of rule following. I don't know what grade I am in, but I don't believe I'm in the first grade any longer, and I'm so thankful for the forgiveness and opportunity to learn how to love like Jesus, and I'm looking forward to advancing to the next grade. At the same time, I'm remorseful for the pain I caused while I was in the first grade of the school of Jesus. This kind of relational faith is exciting to me and is far better than some of the past ideas of rule following I had. We can be thankful that our faith really is about God loving us so much that He offers forgiveness for when we miss the mark, and He wants to teach us how to love like His Son.

That's the bottom line. When I don't love like Him, I am forgiven and given the opportunity to learn how to do better. As we will see in other chapters, this truth plays out a little bit differently in our relationships with each other in how forgiveness and/or restoration of relationships and love plays out after missing the mark with each other, taking on a little different look. But we still learn how Jesus would teach us to respond like Him.

CHAPTER 7

Repentance

Okay, so we may have to get off the path and into the weeds just a little to grasp this concept. I had heard most of my life that repentance means "to turn" or "to turn from sin." This definition simply isn't accurate and does a disservice to the actual intention the word is meant to convey. So let's look a little closer at this word, which is so vital to our faith ideas. The word *repent* in the Bible comes basically from two Greek words, *metanoeo* and *metamelomai*.

Metanoeo

The word *meta* means "after/with" by itself and "change" when used in a compound word. The word *noeo* is the "faculty of thinking" or "mind." So the word literally means to "change your mind." Change your mind about what? Some form of the word is used thirty-four times in the New Testament. Let's look closer at one verse to try to capture the intended meaning. Acts 2:38 says, "Peter replied, 'Repent and be baptized, every one of you, in the name of Jesus Christ for the forgiveness of your sins. And you will receive the gift of the Holy Spirit.'"

We know that *metanoeo* means "change your mind." The word *baptize* is a transliteration (transcribing letter for letter from the Greek alphabet to the approximate English letter) from the word *baptizo*. From *Strong's Exhaustive Concordance #907:* "to immerse, submerge; to make whelmed (i.e. fully wet); used only (in the New Testament) of ceremonial ablution, especially (technically) of the ordinance of Christian baptism."[3] The word translated "in" here is the Greek word *epi*, which means "on" or "on the basis of." The word *for* here is the Greek word *eis*, which means "into"; this carries the thought of motion toward or into something. So let's look at this verse in a more literal translation. Acts 2:38 says, "Peter replied, change your minds and be immersed, every one of you, on the basis of the name of Jesus Christ into the forgiveness of sins. And you will receive the gift of the Holy Spirit."

More literally, when you change your minds about who Jesus Christ is and what He has done for you, you will then be immersed into the forgiveness of sins and receive His gift of the Holy Spirit. It isn't when we "turn" or "turn from sin" that we receive forgiveness. It is when we change our minds or thinking about Jesus Christ, who He is and what He has done for us, which we could never do for ourselves, that He immerses us in forgiveness. Here is why I believe the idea of "turn" got mixed in with repentance. Acts 3:19 says, "Repent, then, and turn to God, so that your sins may be wiped out, that times of refreshing may come from the Lord."

The Greek word *strepho* means "turn." Then prefixes are attached to the beginning to indicate which kind of turning is involved. A person can turn—turn to, turn from, turn back— and the Greek word is very clear what kind of turning is taking place. In this verse, the Greek word is *epistrepho*, which means to "turn back" or "return." So here listeners are being implored

---

[3] *Strong's Exhaustive Concordance* by James Strong S.T.D., LL.D. 1890 Public Domain.

to change their minds and return to God. We cannot turn back to God unless we change our minds about Him first.

True Repentance and Turning

Here is a story of what true repentance and turning look like to me. Imagine I was walking along and fell into a pit of quicksand. In the beginning, it was only up to my knees. Someone behind me said he or she could help me, but I thought I would be able to save myself, so I denied his or her plea to help save me. As I sank farther to my waist, I still ignored his or her plea to save me, but even though I began to struggle more, I still believed I could save myself and wasn't in need of his or her assistance. At some point, when I had sunk up to my chest, I began to change my mind about being able to save myself, so I turned to the person behind me and said I had changed my mind. I needed him or her to save me.

Turning gave me no power to save myself. The turning was just the result of changing my mind about my ability to save myself; I was now entirely dependent on someone else to save me. I now had to stop struggling and submit myself to the one who was able to save me. A change of mind led me to turn back to the one who could save me and be entirely dependent on him or her to be saved. Now, had I been more prepared for this dilemma. Had studied the dangers of quicksand and had read, understood and believed the stories of others who had shared their experiences of being trapped in quicksand, then maybe I would have taken up the offer more quickly before I came to the end of my own resources and submitted to the reality of the truth, because I refused to accept any new ideas about the dangers of quicksand beforehand. Or maybe I was so dependent on my own ideas, which I brought into the situation, and had to exhaust all the ideas I thought would save me. Or I suppose I could have been so independent that I could have suffered the consequences of rejecting the only one who was truly able to save me. Or maybe out of stubborn pride and selfishness, determined to do things my own way, I perished, having never changed my mind about the truth of the circumstances.

Sound familiar?

Metamelomai

The Greek word *metamelomai* is the other word translated "repent," but it has a drastically different meaning. As we have learned, *meta* means "change" when used in compound words. The Greek word *melo*, when used with *meta*, means "to care afterward" or "regret"—literally, a "change of emotions." *Metamelomai* is used in Matthew 27:3 (KJV). "Then Judas, which had betrayed him, when he saw that he was condemned, repented himself, and brought again the thirty pieces of silver to the chief priests and elders."

Many have used the word *repentance* to indicate that Judas had changed his mind about what he had done. But in truth, he had a change of emotions or regretted what he had done. Now, was this change of emotion or regret due to a new understanding of what he had done or regret because he had been caught? I believe verses 4 and 5 (KJV) make this clearer. "Saying, I have sinned in that I have betrayed the innocent blood. And they said, what *is that* to us? see thou *to that*. And he cast down the pieces of silver in the temple, and departed, and went and hanged himself."

These verses indicate that he understood what he had done—"betrayed the innocent blood," which indicates that he had indeed changed his mind about what he had done and was so remorseful that he threw the money back and committed suicide. There are debates as to whether Judas was allowed union with the Father, entrance into heaven, because of his betrayal. Some lean toward his being immersed in the same gift of forgiveness after his regret and understanding what he had truly done and then changing his mind about who Jesus was. Then he received the same salvation any of us undeservedly receive. After all, which of us hasn't betrayed Jesus Christ in like manner, being responsible for Him needing to be nailed on a cross on our behalf? We absolutely couldn't achieve what was needed to satisfy even one "missing of the mark"? John 17:12 however, seems to indicate Judas was still lost. "None has been lost except the one doomed to destruction so that Scripture would be fulfilled." I personally lay down my hammer and leave this one up to a holy, righteous, and loving God.

Repentance and Love

Now let's bring this whole idea of repentance around to the purpose of this book. The two ideas of repentance closely resemble the way God asks us to operate in love, from understanding phileo love (a love of the emotions) to understanding agape love (a love of the mind or will). *Metanoeo* operates from our faculty of thinking or the mind. It requires new ideas to be received and evaluated for their value. When we see the value of the new Kingdom ideas, we will repent, change our minds, sell the old ideas, and hold on to the new ones. *Metamelomai* engages our hearts or emotions when we have missed the mark in our relationship with God, others, or ourselves, and it causes regret and sorrow. Both operating together should move us in the right direction in all our relationships. But wouldn't it be better for all if we sought ("Seek, and Ye shall find" [Matthew 7:7 KJV]) after the right ideas so we could change our minds based on missing the mark of loving God, others, and ourselves, instead of needing to be brought to a point of regret or sorrow because we realized we had missed the mark?

CHAPTER 8

Consequences ... Restorative or Retributive?

Have you ever heard of this debate? Are biblically based consequences restorative or retributive? In other words, are the consequences of missing the mark meant to restore us or to render an "eye for an eye" (Exodus 21:24), which is what we deserve? Here are some of my thoughts concerning this. I believe the initial goal of God's allowing consequences to happen is to restore us to a right relationship with Him, others, and ourselves. God will spend your lifetime trying to conform you to the image of His Son. That process must start with a changing of the mind (repentance). Then God has something to work within your thinking processes.

But if we, at the end of this life, haven't changed our minds about Him and His Son, then we have chosen for ourselves to suffer the consequences of not changing our minds or of unbelief. We can choose to receive what we deserve, although it's difficult for me to understand why anyone would want to take this route if they did it with understanding. Let's look at this issue regarding the human legal system. The whole intent of any penal system is initially to help the offender know there are consequences for not relating to others appropriately. And hopefully, those consequences will offer the offender better ideas of what living appropriately in relation to others is all about. There may come a point in a person's life when a judge or jury has determined that the offender isn't willing to be restored to proper relationships with others and must suffer the consequence of never being restored or doing life in prison. Remember that life means union, and someone, because of his or her choices, will be sentenced to union with a prison, and with others who have made similar choices, instead of the original union with others (separation) or freedom to make better choices. I understand there are exceptions to any rule, such as mental illness, but I speak in general terms or the norm.

I believe God's idea of consequences is for the restoration of mankind to Himself and each other. And any loving authority will allow or designate consequences for the good of the offender and the offended alike. When people play on any sports team and aren't playing the game well, they are taken out of the game to reflect on how they were playing the game, and later they are allowed to try again. When people don't do life well in their union with others, they sometimes need to be taken out of the game to allow the consequences to change their minds, hopefully in a way that might restore them to union with society and protect society from any further offense.

Time-Out

We all understand this principle when it comes to our children. Most parents have employed some version of a time-out or grounding to mete out a measured consequence to protect other children and teach valuable lessons to young offenders. If at some point the young offenders aren't able or willing to play well with others, they aren't allowed to return to union with them (separation). Those who will choose to remain unrepentant and don't change their minds about who God and Jesus are or don't learn to live in a proper relationship with Him and others may choose for themselves the final idea of separation from Him and others in this life and the next. Not what God would choose for them but what they would choose for themselves. His love compels Him to hold up mirrors and allow consequences to restore us to a proper relationship with Him and others, but He allows us opportunities to make these decisions. After all, if obeying Him is a measure of our love for Him, then isn't disobedience a measure of our lack of love for Him? And if we make conscious choices not to love Him, why would He make us do so if His purpose is to teach us how to love like Jesus? Just remember that God is all wise and all knowing, and He takes into account everything within us that causes us to make the decisions we do.

I'm Compelled!

We are all so different in what compels us to make the choices we do and what in our souls and makeup causes us to make the decisions we do. Only God can know what is truly in someone's heart and soul to be able to make these decisions about consequences concerning the next life. But for this life, we have laws based on relational ideas God originally gave, and when we violate these laws, there will be earthly consequences to bear—initially to protect others and restore the offender; but consequences will increase with more offenses, even to the point that restoration is no longer an option. Which is the right, loving response to protect those the offender would offend and teach offenders they aren't allowed to offend others.

So to sum it up, God's intentions are to restore us to a right relationship with Him and others, but we must be careful not to allow ourselves to attain a reprobate mind, a mind that is no longer able to tell right from wrong. If we have that mind, God removes His hands from us—initially in this life for restoration and possibly in the next life because we have chosen to be separated from Him.

CHAPTER 9

Basic Human Needs

Our basic human needs have been the basis of many writings, both Christian and non-Christian—from Maslow's hierarchy of needs to Anthony Robbins's "Basic Human Needs" to Father Thomas Keating's identification of emotional needs. But they all have one similarity: trying to gain an understanding of the basic makeup and needs of the human soul.

I highly recommend looking further into these ideas. A better understanding of what the soul's basic needs are, and how we try to get them met in this world, is a basis for understanding how God wants to and can meet these same needs within appropriate relationships with Him, others, and ourselves. While I have yet to read an author I agreed with in all his or her findings (except the Bible), so it is with these authors I am going to mention.

Books That Shaped Me

While I have read and gained insight by many, four main books have shaped my ideas and understanding of who I am and how to pursue a proper relationship with God, others, and myself.

1. The Bible: This is the only book and author I agree with 100 percent, and it is my favorite.
2. Dallas Willard, *Renovation of the Heart*: This is not for the faint of heart; it is very deep.
3. David Benner, *The Gift of Being Yourself*: I wish everyone would read this one.
4. Father Thomas Keating, *The Human Condition: Contemplation and Transformation*: This book is the smallest of the four, but it is packed with understandable ideas.

The principles in these four books have changed and continue to guide my understanding and seeking today. The Bible is the standard, and the others help me to gain a deeper understanding and search of God's truths and how they have and should shape our lives.

I like Father Thomas Keating's simple, basic understanding of our basic human emotional and biological needs. "All of us have been through the process of being born and entering this world with three essential biological needs: security and survival, power and control, affection and esteem. Without adequate fulfillment of these biological needs, we probably would not survive infancy. Since the experience of the presence of God is not there at the age we start to develop self-consciousness, these three instinctual needs are all we have with which to build a program for happiness. Without the help of reason to modify them, we build a universe with ourselves at the center, around which all our human faculties revolve like planets around the sun. As a result, any object entering into our universe – another person or event – is judged on the basis of whether it can provide us with what we believe or demand happiness to be."[4] Since the

---

[4] Thomas Keating, *The Human Condition: Contemplation and Transformation* (Snowmass, CO: St. Benedict's Monastery, 1999). 13.

topic of this book is love, I will focus on the ideas of love as a basic need for affection and esteem.

It is an incredible idea to think about how the manner in which we are shown love when we are young, is the measure of how lovable we feel, along with the measure of how valuable we feel we are to others as we grow and give love in a similar manner as we have received it. This goes for both agape love and phileo love. We are all born with a soul that needs to be loved and to know how valuable it is to others. I believe God placed these needs in us for two reasons. First, because He knew He was able to provide it for us. Second, because we live in a broken world, separated from Him because of "missing the mark" (sin), and we will pursue trying to find satisfaction for these needs. Proverbs 19:22 says, "What a person desires is unfailing love."

We all have a deep need to love and to be loved in unconditional ways. I believe this is the reason we relate so well to our animal friends. They have an enormous capacity to seemingly give and receive love. And as good as it may feel to give and receive love from animals in unconditional ways, animal love was never meant to replace the healthy relationships God intended for us to have.

Our Nature

Our human, fallen nature tends to lead us to trying to find the solutions in this world. But when the world doesn't deliver in any lasting way, the Holy Spirit helps us to change our minds (repent), gives us new ideas about how God can meet our needs, and turns us back to the Father for real and lasting solutions. Those who deny how these principles govern our thoughts, ideas, and responses will most certainly be tyrannized in the depths of their souls without any understanding of the source of this tyranny. And any soul affected in this way will also not be in a proper relationship with God, others, himself or herself.

It is incredible to watch these ideas play out in relationships that seem to operate from hidden places. I can't tell you how many times I have heard the phrase "That's just how I am." My normal response to this statement is, "Well, just how you are, is very hurtful to those around you." Whenever our needs aren't being met or are being violated, our natural tendency is to respond in one, or a combination, of the following three relational strategies: attack, avoid, or attach.

Attack

Attacking is the aggressive response when the soul lacks having its needs met or is being violated. The attacker's soul says, "You have hurt me, so I will hurt you back. Or I will hurt you before you hurt me." The attacker cannot follow Matthew 18:15 (YLT). "And if thy brother may sin against thee, go and show him his fault between thee and him alone, if he may hear thee, thou didst gain thy brother." This verse means that if brothers (or sisters) miss the mark in relating to you appropriately, you should go to them and reprove (convince with solid, compelling evidence) them for how they have missed the mark in relating to you. Also, you should express how this offense has made you feel. This confrontation gives them the opportunity to change their minds (repent) about what they have done or said to you and how it made you feel. It offers them the opportunity to "hit the mark" or make the relationship right again.

The attacker, in many cases, seeks to make the relationship right but tries to do so in very wrong, destructive, and manipulative ways. In other cases, however, the attacker merely acts in revenge for what the other person has done or made him or her feel.

Withdraw or Avoid

Withdrawing is the more passive or passive-aggressive response to needs not being met or being violated. The withdrawer's soul says, "You have hurt me, so I will just move away from you" or "I will hurt you back by moving away from you." Sometimes the withdrawer simply doesn't know how to respond or defend himself or herself, so he or she leaves. Other times he or she tries to return the hurt by leaving. Others may not feel valuable enough to stay engaged and may leave because they believe they somehow deserved the way they have been treated. In any case, the withdrawer finds it difficult to engage in a Matthew 18:15 way to help the offender know how he or she has missed the mark and made him or her feel. This also plays out in addictions as the withdrawer avoids dealing with inner feelings through the use of alcohol, drugs, pornography, and so forth or through seemingly healthy avoidance behaviors, such as working too much, playing basketball too much, hunting or fishing too much, or even crocheting too much.

Attach

Attaching is more of an enabling or codependent way of responding to needs not being met or being violated. The attacher's soul says, "If I love you enough, you will love me back." Some would say, "I find my value in how you perceive me." Others would say, "I understand how much you have been through and don't want to make it worse," even though the actions of the attacher may fuel the bad behavior. Engaging in a Matthew 18:15 way isn't even in the attacher's system of response ideas since he or she isn't willing to take a chance on the offender rejecting or hurting him or her further.

I realize these explanations are very basic and can play out in many ways and for many reasons, but my reason for mentioning them is to show how we respond from "who we are" and in ways that seem to come so naturally from our subconscious selves.

All Are Destructive to Relationships

Please understand that all the responses mentioned above are very destructive to relationships. Attackers can destroy a relationship very quickly by saying or doing things they later wish they could take back. Withdrawers destroy relationships more slowly by not staying engaged in any healthy ways that may lead to a healing of the relationship. Attachers harm the relationship by enabling the hurtful behavior of the offender and allowing the relationship to be based on all the wrong things. You may also notice that *attack* and *withdraw* are terms used in battle, which is no coincidence.

The more appropriate way to resolve sins against each other is to stay engaged in a Matthew 18:15 way that says, "I will go to offenders and help them to understand how they have offended me and how they have impacted me." Many times, this situation takes a third party who understands a relationally healthier process or a trained counselor or therapist who can walk him or her through appropriate and safe ways to stay engaged in a manner that may lead to restoring a relationship or putting up boundaries in unsafe, unhealthy ones.

Life Is about Relationships

Anytime we allow ourselves to be involved in relationships of any kind, we make ourselves vulnerable, to varying degrees, of hurting or being hurt, or not having our needs met in the ways our souls deem necessary for our own well-being. The extent to which we understand how to operate in healthy, loving relationships (agape and phileo) is the extent to which we will have success in those relationships. We will all experience the hurts, fears, and frustrations of relationships as we travel through this life. What matters is how we learn to respond to them or whether we just allow who we are at the core to respond in unhealthy ways. We all have some very basic human needs that need to be met, along with the natural elements that are in each of us to varying degrees: "the lust of the flesh, the lust of the eyes, and the pride of life" (1 John 2:16). When the dysfunction of not knowing how to have our basic human needs met in healthy ways mixes with our natural temperament—the natural lusts of the flesh, eyes, and pride—this situation leads to insatiable and addictive behaviors. It is one thing to live in a saved condition, knowing we will spend eternity with the Father when our time comes. It is wholly another to live in spiritual and emotional health because we have learned God's ideas of life and love, and are daily applying that knowledge to our lives and relationships.

CHAPTER 10

The Right Thing for the Right Reason

As discussed earlier, people generally tend to do the right thing for one of two reasons. They understand how their choice, thought or action, doesn't show appropriate love for God, others, or themselves. Or they no longer are willing to pay the price of the consequences their choices might bring. I want to elaborate on this idea of doing the right thing for the right reason because I believe it lies at the heart of our faith. There are differences of opinion as to whether Christ followers should emphasize His justice and righteousness or whether they should emphasize His love and grace. Here are my thoughts on the matter.

I believe it depends. How's that for an opinion? The answer truly depends on who you are speaking to. It depends on the maturity, awareness, understanding, and willingness to hear on the part of the one being spoken to. Let me explain.

One example is my marriage to my wife, Linda. If I promised my wife that I would never have an affair, that would be a good thing, right? But let's examine that idea closer. What if I told her I wouldn't have an affair and followed up with these reasons?

1. I don't want her to divorce me.
2. I don't want to be alone.
3. I don't want to pay child support.

If I gave her these reasons (and trust me, I have heard all these reasons), take a moment to ponder how my reasoning would make my wife feel. Would it make her feel loved and valued? Would it make her think I was acting on her behalf in my choices? Would she sincerely trust that I would do my best to avoid the situation? I don't believe so. This would be an example of doing the right thing for a purely selfish reason. Now, would she take this reasoning over saying I would have an affair? Maybe. But I don't think my reasons would cause her to feel safe or trust me fully.

Now, what if my reasoning were more like this? "I won't have an affair because I understand how much it would hurt you. It would make you feel like I could care less about how you feel. I have pondered what you, as a woman, must have thought throughout your life concerning the kind of man you wanted to call your husband. You danced for your daddy when you were a little girl, and in the innocence of your mind, you said, 'Look at me, Daddy. Love me, Daddy.' And your father handed that little girl to me on our wedding day with the hope that I would love and care for her as he did. I thought about the idea that as that little girl grew, she began to think about who her Prince Charming would be and began thinking about her wedding day. And she even began saving things for her future marriage. That I at least have some idea of how much God made you the relational one, and He gave you to me to learn that softer side of Himself. I never wanted to trample on your idea of who you need me to be, and while I was never meant to take the place of your relationship with God, I was put in your life to love and protect everything about you and to be God's gift in skin to you."

So instead of just telling her, "I won't have an affair," I want her to see the boundaries I am placing around me so that not only will I not have an affair, but I will also try my best to keep myself from being tempted or being in a position where anyone would question my motives. I want her to feel safe and secure, knowing that I don't want to have an affair or be in a position for her or anyone else to question my motives because I love her and have spent time considering these things and would never want to hurt her in that way.

Can you begin to see the difference between doing the right thing for the right reason and doing it for the wrong one? Oh, how I wish someone in my life could have taught me these principles as a young man. Just maybe I would have made different choices when it came to loving and respecting others in appropriate ways. This admission doesn't make me a super husband, just one who is honest about my weaknesses and ability to hurt others. I am trying to learn how to place measures in my life to keep me from falling. Primarily I'm seeking to know and live in the presence of Jesus Christ so He can give me the strength, wisdom, and knowledge to appropriately love Him, others, and even myself.

As a Child

When I was a child, I wanted to help my parents do the chores because that natural gift of relational love in me wanted to be with them and do what they were doing. It was the right thing for the right reason. But there came a time when doing the chores didn't come from my heart, out of love for them. The world's influence and my selfish desires had started taking precedence over what God had naturally intended a loving relationship to look like, and I began to stray by seeking what I thought was best for myself, so my parents laid down a consequence that said, "This is what will happen if you don't do it." A law or rule so to speak. Now, this rule didn't give me any power to follow it, only motivation to do the right thing for the wrong reason.

You see, the law was meant to show us when we miss the

mark. Did my parents wish that I would do the chores because I loved them and knew how valuable it was to do my part in the family dynamics? Sure. But that wasn't in my understanding at that point. You might say I was immature in my thinking and understanding. So they did the only thing they knew to teach me the lessons they wanted me to learn about being part of the family. But as I grew, they began to teach me about taking my place in the family for the right reasons. Paul said something similar in First Corinthians 13:11–13 (NASB). "When I was a child, I used to speak like a child, think like a child, reason like a child; when I became a man, I did away with childish things. For now we see in a mirror dimly, but then face to face; now I know in part, but then I will know fully just as I also have been fully known. But now faith, hope, love, abide these three; but the greatest of these is love."

I believe Paul was saying that in his immaturity he thought and reasoned with an immature understanding. But when he became a man, who was more mature, he began laying aside his childish, immature thoughts and started considering and doing the right thing for the right reason. Remember that these verses are found within what we call "the love chapter." Paul gave quite a dissertation on what love is and isn't. He went on to talk about "seeing in a mirror dimly." A more literal interpretation would be a dirty, clouded mirror. When God holds a mirror up to us, it's hard for us to see who we really are because of the worldliness and dirty filter we are looking through. "But then face to face" tells us that when we come into His presence, we will see Him face-to-face, and we will see a perfect reflection of who we truly are, without all the dirt. We will see what real, perfect love looks like because we will look at His face and see a reflection of perfect love, who He made us to be; a beautiful image of truth. And love is the greatest attribute of all that remains.

Applying These Ideas

Now with those ideas in mind, think for a moment of me saying that I believe in Jesus Christ because His righteousness demands that I believe and follow the laws, or I will experience the consequence of unbelief and disobedience in the next life. Could this be the right thing for the wrong reason? That I profess something, much the way I did to my wife, for purely selfish reasons? That I didn't want to experience the consequence of my choices, so I professed a belief? Would God take this motive as true repentance? In my thinking, it's possible that a mind so immature and unaware of what God has done for us, and so unaware of how to make choices from agape love, would need to be motivated by consequences, but is that true repentance and faith?

Imagine that you were the strongest, toughest, nicest, and the most considerate person on the face of the planet. Imagine that I was going to tell some friends of mine why they should be friends with you. Would you want me to try to scare them into a relationship with you by starting with how easily you could destroy them if they didn't become your friend? Is this the kind of relationship you would like to have with them, one based on a fear of consequences if they don't act right toward you? Or would you want me to tell them how loving, thoughtful, and considerate you are? And begin that relationship on what is most important about you?

Now I understand that if they didn't care about how they treated you or how much you cared about them, it would be in their best interest to know what the consequences would be. So I would never say that part of the conversation is off the table, just not the beginning or the emphasis of my description of you. And I also realize that they should know that even though you are so kind and loving, you still have the ability to crush them, but your love for them calls them into a relationship that will be good for them and protect and care for them. So I understand that consequences have a place and time, but they should never be the primary description of who God is.

In Practice

For believers, Jesus Christ died on our behalf because we could never satisfy that righteousness and justice. And because of our relationship with Christ, we don't need to worry about the consequences of such things. For unbelievers, God sent His Son to die for them as well. And they need to understand His love for them, that Jesus died to take their place, and that He longs to be in a loving relationship with them, care for them, and bring them into an everlasting relationship with the Father. These truths should motivate them to seek out His friendship and all that is offered through a relationship with Jesus Christ.

But if they are hard-hearted and set on their selfish ways, there is a consequence of separation from all He is and can be, to and for them. But think for a moment about how we must make God sometimes feel when we try to scare people into a relationship with Him by emphasizing the consequences of not accepting His love. God is love, and He pursues us all from who He is. God loving us should always be the primary conversation, and the secondary conversation would be what He could do to us. He wants us to love Him back for who He is and what He has done for us, and if we refuse to do so, I am sure He would like us to know what we have chosen instead.

Don't Get a Ticket

Another example of this idea is the dreaded traffic stop for speeding. Generally speaking, we all hate it when a police officer pulls us over. But stop and think about this for a moment. If you are driving down the road and see a sign that shows the speed limit to be fifty-five miles per hour, why would you obey it? Most of us would say we obey because we don't want to get a speeding ticket, but that is doing the right thing for the wrong reason or at least a selfish one. The right reason should be because I understand someone did a study and determined that the safest speed for all concerned is fifty-five. And because I desire to show appropriate love to those around me and myself, I should follow the speed limit. Tickets are written to those who decide not to drive with others first in their considerations; they need consequences to remind them that they are violating their relationship with others. Think about it. Aren't all laws man has made based on the different ways we choose not to live within appropriate relationships with each other? If we all knew how to live in a right relationship with those around us and put forth the efforts to do so, we wouldn't need any laws. But since some either don't understand how or don't care, we must put laws in place to show everyone when he or she is missing the standard and that there will be consequences for missing it, but the primary goal is always appropriate relationships with those around us.

God's Word

The New Testament gives a similar picture. It shows us so many different ways we miss the mark (sin) in our relationships with God, each other, and even ourselves. The Bible was never meant to be a book of rules but a mirror to show us when we don't love properly. We don't always know how to look into it, or we simply don't want to.

The moral of this chapter is to take time to consider why we do what we do or why we don't do what we don't do. It is to seek not just to follow a set of rules but to understand how the rules are intended to protect relationships. And with enough consideration of the principle behind the law, maybe we will do the right thing for the right reason and teach others as well. This principle applies to how we relate to God and man. And if we don't do the right thing for the right reason, God or man may need to impose consequences to teach us a lesson. The problem is, we can never be good enough for God or man to follow all the rules, and we need to be taught the principles behind the laws, so we begin to understand what it means to be in a proper relationship with God, others, and ourselves.

Summing It Up

So when we tell others about this God we claim to know, wouldn't the best way be to teach them to do the right thing for the right reasons? That God loves them so much that He gave His only Son to die on their behalf so they would never have to be separated from that love? That He will continue to pursue them in spite of their indifference to Him? That He provided a way for us not to have to suffer the consequences of our choices and that He wants to teach us how to love and live in a proper relationship with Him and others? And that if they choose not to accept His love, there are consequences of being separated from the one who created them? There are endless ways to try to teach others about the love of God, the best is an example of what that love looks like, and this should be our emphasis.

It's hard to show others how much you love them when you are threatening them with the consequences. Maybe, just maybe, if they think you generally care about them, they will listen to your concern for their safety and well-being. But these conversations must always be held in a manner that says: "I care about you and don't want to see you hurt." Not from a self-righteous need to be right or from carelessly going around and condemning everyone with an attitude that you really don't care about him or her or that you care more about standing for what you know. This is the reason Jesus broke the law when He healed on the Sabbath. He wanted to show the higher law of love and that living in a proper loving relationship with the Father is a 24-7 proposition, not just setting aside one day a week to recognize Him. Being freed from the law was to teach us that there was no power in following it. The power He gives us is in learning how to love like He does. And that, my friends, is a lifelong adventure.

CHAPTER 11

My Good Friend, Jesus

Have you ever had a friend you dearly loved and respected? Then one day you met someone else for the first time who had a close relationship with this friend and loved him or her equally. You began sharing your experiences of this friend with the other person, and you shared your opinion about your friend and the things you knew, had seen, or had heard about him or her. Somehow the stories didn't quite line up with each other, and your ideas of this person were a bit different. You and the other person may have had some disagreement about your opinions of your mutual friend, but that didn't mean you both didn't love your friend equally. And even if you disagreed vehemently about an attribute of this friend, after trying to prove the other person wrong, you both contacted the friend's spouse and asked questions, seeking the truth, you both still came up with different ideas about what the spouse conveyed concerning your mutual friend. Here are a couple of thoughts here:

1. Do you believe your mutual friend, whom you both love, would want you arguing and dividing over your ideas and experiences of him or her?
2. Is it possible, as you share your ideas and experiences, that you might get a better, bigger picture of who your

friend is? As you meet others who know your mutual friend well through engaging conversation, this picture might grow in a way that you have a much better understanding of who your friend is because of these conversations than you could ever have experienced in your relationship with him or her alone.

In Like Manner

I do believe our relationship with the Father, Son, and Holy Spirit should be similar to this picture. As we share our understanding and experiences through respectful but engaging conversation, we should be able to get a better overall picture of who our God is. And it should be much better than we could understand through only our relationship with Him.

Is there a truth about our ideas we should be seeking? Absolutely! The Bible is equivalent to asking the spouse who knows Him the best. Is there absolute truth that should be gleaned from questioning God's word for the truth? Possibly, but I don't personally know any person or religion I believe is so holy and in tune with God that he or she can discern all truth. Besides, I don't think God designed us to be able to determine all truth on our own. He made us to be in an appropriate, loving relationship with Him, each other, and even ourselves. So together we should be able to show the world a bigger picture of the one we say we all love.

Instead, we often see arguing and dissension—separation from each other—because we are so sure we know Him perfectly and feel the need to make everyone else conform to our understanding of the truth. I believe this is where God designed the rubber to meet the road in being able to look at people and tell whether they are Christians. Those who are genuinely seeking and learning to be like Jesus Christ. John 13:34–35 says it this way: "A new command I give you: love one another. As I have loved you, so you must love one another. By this everyone will know that you are my disciples, if you love one another."

All three uses of the word *love* in these verses were translated from a form of the word *agape*. That is a commitment to using the mind and will to try always to do what is best for all concerned, even though my heart or emotions may prompt me to do otherwise. Yes, I understand that if I believe I know and understand truth better than someone else, the loving thing to do is to try to help him or her understand this truth. But this should never happen at the cost of unloving behavior, name calling, or belittling of the other person because he or she disagrees. I have personally witnessed this kind of behavior in the name of standing up for the truth while the person left hurt and destruction in his or her path.

This hurt and destruction aren't at all what God had in mind for His followers when they disagree. They should try to stay engaged in a way to share their differences. They should care enough about the one they disagree with to remain in some form of a relationship with him or her and still have influence. If the disagreement is so vehement that this isn't possible, then separation is necessary but not in the manner in which enemies would separate. I also understand that we may have concerns that others are spreading things we may determine to be detrimental to the good of some. This can be like walking a tightrope because I do believe we have a responsibility to share what we believe to be the truth. But once we have been told that others don't accept what we are saying and reject what we offer to be the truth, then there are a couple of ways we would stay in line with showing agape love to those we vehemently disagree with.

1. We could separate from them without trying to destroy them or their character. Remember, just because I may

disagree doesn't automatically make me right. And it never gives me the right to treat brothers and sisters in Christ, whom we are obligated to show agape love to, in a manner that would tear them down. And never forget that the world is watching. And if Jesus said the world would know us by our love for one another, then those outside the faith will judge us accordingly. Do we expect them to want to take up our banner of love when it is riddled with hate? I understand that there are consequences for not knowing the truth, and we would be remiss if we didn't remind people of those consequences. But this is after engaging, respectful conversations, and it should always take place in a manner that we are exhibiting the reason we are sharing the consequences with them. And that is because we care about them and don't want them to suffer these consequences. Even our God doesn't take away their right to be wrong. We should always strive to offer the truth in love, evaluating how we are perceived by outsiders and where we may or may not be practicing the love of God in our efforts to stand for truth. These traits of self-awareness and honesty with oneself are rare today.

2. We can and should try to manage our emotions in a way that would allow us to stay engaged in the process and still have influence. Oh, and this process might cause us to seek deeper because we are trying to find ways to show them the truth, and we may learn more about the truth in this process. Don't you think our political system would benefit greatly from these practices as well?

Contending for the Faith

I have often seen this verse quoted in defense of standing vehemently for the truth: Jude 1:3 says, "Dear friends, although I was very eager to write to you about the salvation we share, I felt compelled to write and urge you to contend for the faith that was once for all entrusted to God's holy people."

But I believe this verse often is used and quoted out of context of the verses that follow it. Verse 4 sums up the preceding verses and explains who they were contending against. Jude 1:4 says, "For certain individuals whose condemnation was written about long ago have secretly slipped in among you. They are ungodly people, who pervert the grace of our God into a license for immorality and deny Jesus Christ our only Sovereign and Lord."

Whoever chooses to use Jude 1:3 to justify their unloving disagreements with others should always make sure the target of their godly arrows meets the two qualifications pointed out in verse 4.

1. "They are ungodly people, who pervert the grace of our God into a license for immorality."
2. "And [they] deny Jesus Christ our only Sovereign and Lord."

Let us, please be careful whom we place into this category and be sure they are deserving of the consequences that follow, or those believing they are doing the right thing may do severe damage to the Kingdom.

CHAPTER 12

Taking the Logs Out of Our Eyes

Luke 6:42 (NASB) says, "Or how can you say to your brother, 'Brother, let me take out the speck that is in your eye,' when you yourself do not see the log that is in your own eye? You hypocrite, first take the log out of your own eye, and then you will see clearly to take out the speck that is in your brother's eye."

Have you ever gone to a sporting venue or theater, only to be seated behind the large pillar that obstructs your view? This is how Luke described the log in this verse. And the speck was a splinter compared to the log. Similar statements today would be the following:

- Look in the mirror before you point out someone else's faults.
- Clean your own house before criticizing another's.
- If you stop focusing on other people's lives, you will have time to fix your own.
- Sweep first before your own door before you sweep the doorsteps of your neighbors.

There are probably hundreds of similar statements we have heard throughout our lives, yet how many take time to consider how these statements affect our relationships and examine their own lives before offering advice or criticism to others? Who is willing to receive your input about their splinter, because they believe you have agape love for them when they can see this huge beam stuck in your eye, obstructing your view? That would be akin to hiring overweight, out-of-shape fitness instructors to help me meet my health goals. Even if they had some knowledge to share concerning my fitness, I wouldn't want to hear it from them since I would find it hard to accept that they really believe it themselves. And how could they show me what is in my best interest when they struggle with doing what is in their own best interest? I believe most of us are willing to take advice concerning just about anything if two conditions are in place.

1. We believe others have our best interest in mind (agape love).
2. They have proved what they say to be true by first living it out or experiencing the advice in their own life.

Whether they have strong feelings toward us (phileo love) may or may not make any difference to us if these two parts exist in the exchange of information. It helps if the advice comes from someone who is emotionally invested in us and has our best interest at heart. But we don't need our fitness instructor to care about us with phileo love, although it may feel better.

I believe the depth of these ideas is rarely considered in relationships. How we relate to each other in matters of disagreement, hurtful interactions, or desires to have our deepest needs met rarely includes a process of self-examination before offering our opinions of how the other person has offended or "missed the mark."

Intimate relationships manifest these ideas with more intensity than others due to our allowing ourselves to be emotionally vulnerable to others and the extent to which we place the responsibility of meeting our basic human needs on others. How we understand these concepts and practice looking first in the mirror has often made the difference between healthy growing relationships and divorce (literally the death of a marriage). So here are some ideas I have learned and strived to practice concerning the speck and log concept.

Looking Back

Growing up, I was blessed to be raised by two parents who always sought to provide for me and keep me safe. Both parents were extremely hard working, caring people who loved their family and exhibited love for others. I loved them very much. No one should take the following statements out of this context. As good as my parents were, they weren't Jesus Christ, meaning they weren't perfect. I think we can agree that perfect people don't exist, meaning that perfect parents don't exist, and neither do perfect children. My mother lost her father to divorce at a young age and lost her mother to death at the age of thirteen. I don't think it's too difficult to understand how these losses could cause someone to struggle emotionally when trying to be in healthy yet vulnerable relationships. My father grew up on the streets of the west side of Kansas City, a predominantly Hispanic area with a reputation for its toughness.

It's quite amazing to see how well my parents did in life considering how their younger days formed them. I can only speak for my own experience as I have a brother and sister who had their own experiences while growing up. But for some reason I cannot fully explain today, I didn't feel complete in the amount of love and value my soul thought it needed. It's very difficult to quantify how much of this was because of my parents' emotional inability to meet those needs in me or whether my soul had a stronger-than-normal craving for these things because of my God-given temperament. (Don't worry. I am not going to get off on that rabbit trail. You're welcome.) I imagine the reason was some combination of the two.

I have come to realize from this, that I can misread intentions and quite easily feel hurt by others, especially in my more intimate relationships. This issue has caused struggles in my marriage, especially during the first few years, since I had subconsciously placed a heavy burden on my wife to meet the basic needs of love and value in me. The problem is, I had placed a burden on her she could never meet, and when she failed, she was the problem, and I verbally attacked her. Honestly, I don't understand why she ever stayed with me during those hurtful years. When I asked her, she just said she had seen something more in me and believed in me. I don't want to minimize this response at all; however, there was also the idea that she didn't fully know how to be in a healthy relationship, which helped her to stay with me, because if she had been emotionally healthy, as she is now, she would have been more likely to leave me. You might say we were "equally yoked" and grew together. Here are some of the life-and-love lessons I have learned from all this:

- Before I learned to look in the mirror before responding to a perceived hurt, much of my responses to her was from the burden I had placed on her to meet my needs to be loved and valued; it wasn't always based solely on what she had done. But my soul couldn't tell the difference. The hurt was deep and my soul demanded that I do something to fix it. This pressure in my soul to meet my soul's basic needs led me to alcohol at a young age. It seemed to ease the pressure for a time but soon became the thing I had placed the burden on to meet my needs. When I got married, while I was still drinking at the time, I transferred part of that burden to my wife.
- Much like Adam, God created me with these basic human needs because He was fully capable of meeting

them, and being the essence of love; He longed to meet them all.

• I spoke in an earlier chapter about God's interaction with Adam in the garden, and this carries more ideas here. As God looked at Adam one day, He made a remarkable statement. He said, "It is not good for man to be alone, I will make a helper suitable for him" (Genesis 2:18). The reason this is so remarkable is that God was right there walking with Adam. Adam wasn't alone. I see this as God saying that Adam didn't know how to let Him be everything for him and meet all his basic human needs. What an incredibly loving and humble statement to make from the one who had all to give, but Adam didn't know how to receive it. So God gave him a helper. I strongly believe that God loved him so much that He gave him something to make up the difference of what he couldn't receive until God took him home to be with Himself, where he would know how to let God be his everything and meet all his needs. So now here is this helper or woman in his life, given by God to help him not feel alone. We know the story of them missing the first mark of not loving God appropriately by eating the forbidden fruit. When Adam and Eve heard God "walking in the garden in the cool of the day" (Genesis 3:8), they hid from Him.

Then God started the process of asking man to look in the mirror. He asked, "Where are you?" (Genesis 3:9). Now think about that question for a moment. The God of the universe, who is all knowing, asked them, "Where are you?" when He obviously knew right where they were and why they were hiding. So why did He ask? He wanted Adam and Eve to look in the mirror He held up to them. To see where they were in relation to Him and to see He was the God who loved them unconditionally; they were hiding from Him. There will most certainly be negative consequences when we unlovingly disobey God and hide from Him. Did Adam look in this mirror God was holding up to him? No! He blamed Eve. And so his unloving ways now extended to his helper, and he blamed her for the choice he had made. He threw her under the garden bus.

As I read about the consequences of not loving God properly, I found a fascinating concept I had never been taught. The consequence for Eve is described in Genesis 3:16. "I will make your pains in childbearing very severe; with painful labor you will give birth to children. Your desire will be for your husband, and he will rule over you."

"Your desire will be for your husband." Does this mean, part of her consequence will be that she will be the relational one? "I will make you so relational that you will feel the depth of the pain of broken relationships." I believe Eve, representing God to make up the difference for Adam, must now feel the pain of broken relationships as God does. He placed a relational piece of Himself in Eve. Is this not the natural inclination of most women? I realize that in this fallen world we live in today, life and formation can change these natural inclinations, but for the most part, I believe women live with the consequences of the pain of broken relationships. They are naturally more relational than men. But men, if they want to learn to have agape love in their relating, must learn this part of God from Him, and the woman.

A Dilemma

Now, here is the problem with all this. Because we don't know how to let God be our everything and meet all our needs, we struggle to understand how much we seek to have God meet them and how much we assign to others or things to make up the difference. Only a deeper and more intimate relationship with Jesus Christ can show us where we have assigned too much responsibility to another or "stuff" and not given to God what belongs to Him. We are all dysfunctional in this area. I think it would serve us all better if we spent time with a spiritual leader and/or Christian therapist who could help us look in the mirror to see why we do what we do and where we are assigning the satisfying of our needs to someone or something that may belong to God.

Sorting It Out

Here is a method I often use while learning to look into this relational mirror. Whenever we feel offended, there are two basic things we are looking for.

1. How much of the responsibility truly lies with someone else for the offense?
2. How much of the responsibility lies with me to look in the mirror and see where my wounds may be getting touched?

Sometimes people genuinely offend us intentionally. Much of the time, the offense involves the touching of a previous wound this person had nothing to do with. It's kind of like having an open cut on your arm. There are those who would intentionally poke their finger in it to see you wince. Others may accidentally brush against it, making you wince. Either way, your reaction will be in proportion to the pain felt and the perceived intent to cause it.

So one way to try to determine what responsibility belongs to others and what belongs to you is to imagine a scale of one to ten; try to assign a value to the offense. On a scale of one to ten, was the offense a five, six, or seven? Here is a real-life scenario I had to work through a few years ago and still have to be aware of.

At the time, my wife was working a full-time job. Her routine was generally to be home by six o'clock in the evening. Whenever she wasn't home at six, I allowed my thoughts to run wild. The farther past six the clock displayed, the more frustrated and angry I became. Finally, I called her and let her know how rude and insensitive her actions were, with maybe an expletive thrown in here and there to bolster my manipulative tactics. This was just me responding in the only way I knew how. "That's just the way I am."

Rabbit trail: This idea of just being the way I am is one of the most common excuses for lack of loving behavior. I sometimes use a water bottle as an example. I take the lid off and place pressure on the sides of the bottle while asking, "If I squeeze this bottle hard enough, what will come out?"

The typical response is "water."

Then I ask, "Why does water come out when I put pressure on it?"

"Because that's what was in there."

We cannot expect anything but water to come out, no matter how hard we try. If water is in there, then water will come out when pressure is applied. If we want something else to come out, don't we need to put something else in the bottle? We are similar to water bottles; whenever pressure has been applied to our souls, whatever is in there will come out. Our souls are a product of the sum of what was poured into us, along with our God-given temperament (a book in itself, which thankfully others have written) — our souls' ideas of how to be loved and valued come from the ideas poured into us. If we want something different to come out of us, then we need to put new ideas of love and value in us. End of rabbit trail; I will move on now.

When I began learning how to try to quantify responsibility for this offense, I learned to examine it from an agape and phileo perspective. On a scale of one to ten, how severe did my feelings tell me the offense was (phileo or emotional)? A one means a light offense, and a ten means one of the worse things someone could do to me. I assigned the offense with a phileo seven. Then I had to engage my mind and understanding (agape or mind). I asked myself, How severe should this offense really be? From an intellectual view or a practical and safety view? I then assigned the offense with an agape three, meaning that if she were going to be later than usual, the considerate and loving thing would reasonably be to call or text and let me know, so I didn't need to wonder. There was the possibility that something could happen to her on her way home, and if she was late, I should have looked for her. So if I assigned a phileo of seven and agape of three, then three of the offense belonged to her. And guess what? Four belonged to me. I learned this was a log in my eye that wouldn't allow me to see the situation clearly. I then began trying to look in the mirror to understand why I had a four in this situation and only talked to her about her three responsibilities.

You notice I said, "Talked to her." When I walked through this scenario in an agape and phileo way, I had to take responsibility for my four, which took most of the emotions out of the issue, and I could approach her at a level three instead of a level-seven intensity. Through this managing of emotions, I was able to explain how what she was doing impacted me. And I was also able to learn about my fears of abandonment, which were part of my four, and the other part was responding how I knew to respond. (I know. You don't have to tell me how messed up I am.)

So I explained these things to her as well, and instead of getting a defensive response from her for my coming at her at a level seven, she responded with, "I am sorry. I never meant to make you feel that way." A remarkable change. We no longer fought about this issue but had productive conversations on how to love each other appropriately and do what is best for each other. I also began learning how to understand God's word in a way that helped me to deal with my fears of abandonment so I could learn to trust Him for these things and not place the burden on my wife to make me feel safe and secure. I also learned (and am still learning) to act toward my wife with agape love, trying to do what is best and appropriate for her in spite of how I am feeling (phileo). This process has become my go-to process for dealing with offenses in my life and is still teaching me how to let God be God, and meet my needs in as much as my understanding and will, know how today. And I will keep searching for more understanding, letting my wife be who she is (hopefully going through a similar process so who she is, isn't hurtful to me) and not placing so much burden on her to meet my needs, just letting her make up the difference. And when I place too much burden on her that belongs to God, I must remember that she isn't God and can meet only so much of my soul's basic human needs. And I am learning not to set her up for failure, for which my soul prompts me to attack for my own well-being.

When two people commit to a process of looking in the mirrors God holds up to them and taking the logs out of their eyes so they can see clearly, it is much easier to receive from each other, those things that used to cause division and help them work toward having agape love for each other. Making it so much easier to keep the heart engaged (phileo love).

CHAPTER 13

Addictive Behaviors

One might ask what a chapter like this is doing in a book explaining biblical love. The basis of addiction of any kind is how we play God for ourselves. Much like Adam, we have a propensity not to know how to let God meet our needs with what and whom He has provided, so we look to this world to try to meet the needs for ourselves. In our humanness, we have a tendency to look at others, things, or situations and evaluate them based on their ability to meet our basic needs, when we should be seeking how God can meet them by what He has provided. While He uses others, things, or situations to help make up the difference, when we place the wrong emphasis on these things to meet our needs, they become our gods; our source of dependence.

The problem is, God gave them to us to make up the difference, and They seem to have some short-term ability to satisfy the soul, thinking its needs are being completely met by them when in reality we are becoming more and more dependent on their presence to sustain our sense of well-being. A recipe for addictive behavior and dependence on the wrong things. Jeremiah 2:13 describes the problem this way: "My people have committed two sins: They have forsaken me, the spring of living water, and have dug their own cisterns, broken cisterns that cannot hold water."

I have a really simple idea for what I call a problem as it pertains to addictive behavior. Is something causing a problem in your relationship with God, others, or yourself? If so, then it is a problem. I had a couple in my office because the man drank one beer a day after work, and his wife believed this practice was a sin. After much listening, I asked the man a simple question. "Is drinking one beer a day causing a problem in your relationship with God, anyone around you, or with yourself?"

He answered, something like, "It's a problem with her."

I responded, "If drinking is causing a problem in your relationship, then you have a drinking problem. It doesn't mean you are an alcoholic. It means your relationship has a problem, and the source of that problem is apparently you drinking one beer a day. Or is it? Let's talk this through and try to understand each other. Then maybe you can find some middle ground as a solution."

You see, conflict resolution happens when both parties listen to each other closely enough to understand why the other person feels the way he or she does, even if the other person doesn't agree. When both parties have a better understanding of the other, then the stage is set for compromise. We were able to achieve this compromise through discussions as they listened to each other for the first time.

Then you have those who indeed have become dependent on something other than God to meet some internal need. This is when a person generally needs help thinking through the situation to find a healthy direction to go.

Overcoming

The basis for learning how to overcome our addiction to the wrong things isn't improving our ability to say no, which is legalism in its purest form. It is learning how to focus on what we will allow ourselves to say yes to. If I continually try to say no to what I'm trying not to do, then I am so focused on it that I will eventually give into it. My focus needs to be on my understanding of what needs I'm trying to get met and on where to meet them in Godly, healthy ways. These become my yeses, which I must focus on. As I get better and better at defining my yeses and learning Godly, healthy ways to meet these needs, I find that I spend less time trying to tell myself no.

Now please understand that addictions can get to the point where the body and mind are so dependent on the thing meeting our needs that we aren't able to process our way through all this, and we need to come out of the game for a period. We may even be helped with some form of medication to help us process in healthier ways. Addiction counselors, programs, and licensed therapist are often needed to get the mind and body in a place to be able to work through these truths in a way the mind and soul can respond in healthy ways. Addiction isn't the focus of this book, but I believe we are all addicted to some form of idea processing or behavior that is destructive and unloving to our relationship with God, others, and ourselves. So understanding these principles is beneficial for all of us.

A New Thought

I want to offer you a new idea to consider. I know many people have been told they will never overcome their addictive behavior by trying to do so for others; they must do so for themselves. I suppose this is because they have watched many fail when trying to overcome their addictions for others. I suggest that the reason they failed isn't that they were trying to overcome their addictions for others, but because they were physically and emotionally addicted and needed a better plan of success. I have helped many who were addicted by helping them to see how finding better solutions to the addiction was the loving thing to do for their relationship with God, others, and themselves. They shouldn't do it just for themselves, understanding that the reason they went down this road of self-pleasing behavior and found ways to meet their own needs was due to placing themselves before others. Why would I try to get them to come to a healthier understanding of the process by trying to get them to further focus on doing another thing for themselves above others? Their unhealthy phileo love for themselves sought to meet their own basic human needs for themselves and failed to properly consider agape love in the process, which would have first considered what was best for their relationship with God and others and then themselves. They went down the road of seeking answers to meet their needs so far that they didn't know how to turn back. Now, overcoming for themselves is definitely part of the process; I just believe that if we are supposed to do everything with the priority of loving God first, others, and then self, we will find healing for the good of all three and not just for ourselves. There are more reasons to help us sustain health than just self-motivated ones, which give us a better chance for success.

Those who are so physically and emotionally addicted that they cannot process good information any longer will struggle to overcome their addiction for the good of anyone. And there are certainly those who, because of past wounds, have an unhealthy or distorted view of themselves and others. These need help to stabilize their bodies and thinking processes in a way they can receive good information and ideas, and process them in a way that will be beneficial for all their relationships, including themselves. We must realize that any behavior we become addicted to starts with a process of seeking answers to our felt needs in unhealthy and inappropriate relational ways. The best way to find health is to get the needed help from those who are trained and qualified or have experienced the process for themselves in doing the right things for the right reasons.

If people find sobriety from their addictions and do so for the wrong reasons, they haven't necessarily done the right thing for the right reason, and their relationships may still not find healing. They may just find another behavior to take the place of the old one.

A Day at the Beach

Have you heard of the beach ball theory? If you suppress a beach ball deep enough in the water, it will pop up in another place. Addictions have this same tendency. I know many who found freedom from one addiction, only to find themselves struggling with another one that wasn't healthy for their relationship with God, others, or themselves. Besides, aren't we having these conversations because the people struggling are doing things that aren't good for their relationships with God, others, or themselves? So shouldn't this be the primary motivation for finding freedom? Those are just some thoughts to consider, not rules for overcoming addiction.

My Definition

To sum up this chapter, I offer my basic definition of *addictive behavior*:

> "Continuing the same behavior or action in spite of the consequences of how unloving it is to God, others, or self; and satisfying unmet needs with something from this world instead of from God and what He has provided for physical, mental, emotional, and spiritual health" (Mike G 1:1).

I genuinely believe we are all addicted to behaviors and actions that fit this definition.

Again, I understand that there are those who have become so physically and mentally addicted to something, that ceasing their addiction for any right reason is beyond their ability to achieve. Addictions are powerful. If you are in this place or know someone who is, please seek the help of those who have been trained. Entering Detox is often necessary for those who are so physically addicted that it is not safe for them to try to quit on their own. And interventions are sometimes necessary when a person is incapable of making healthy decisions for others or themselves. Addiction is a very serious matter. There are many who can overcome addiction by learning and applying new ways of thinking, but some have gone too far to will sobriety for themselves, or to allow new ideas to change their behavior.

CHAPTER 14

Relationships

As we can see, our God is a relational God. Everything He wants us to know about Him and life has been given the context of love to operate within. This chapter is where the rubber meets the road. Let's talk about these relationships, and how agape and phileo love look within these relationships our God has defined as being the greatest commandments.

God

When asked what the greatest commandment in the law was, why do you suppose Jesus began by telling us to love God with all our hearts, souls, and minds? I believe He wants us to know that how we relate to others and even ourselves in appropriate ways is a direct result of how we relate to Him. And how we operate within the confines of our various relationships will most certainly be a matter of who we are at the core of our being. And for each of us, that wavering of our hearts, souls, and minds between feelings and willful choices made for the benefit of our own needs and desires or the benefit of others isn't something our natural awareness is programmed to discern. We must learn from the Master. We must become apprentices of love. It is only through learning from the Master that we will be able to promote healthy relationships, work through the difficulties that come along with them, and place proper boundaries around those relationships that aren't healthy.

Hearts, Souls, and Minds

How do we love God with all our hearts? Haven't we come to understand that our hearts are a bit fickle? Jeremiah 17:9 puts it this way: "The heart is deceitful above all things and beyond cure. Who can understand it?"

Has God placed another demand on us we cannot meet? I suppose if we were completely honest with ourselves, we would come to an understanding that in ourselves, how we were formed in a broken world and our natural tendency to look inward, we would conclude that we cannot love God with all our hearts. But we must ask ourselves a question. Is this because we can't, won't, or are unwilling to learn? Probably a mixture of each, but if God is the only one who can understand it, then how do we learn? Oh, I see. I just answered my own question. We learn from Him.

If God is the only one who truly knows and understands our motives, is the Master of relationships, and loves to hold up mirrors to show us who and where we are, then being in the apprenticeship of love is absolutely the only way to learn how to love better. This means I must spend time with the Master, study the ideas He has left me to learn from, and hang around those who have been in this apprenticeship program much longer than I have. One of the most valuable lessons I learned in leadership was that to be a good leader; I didn't always need to know the right answers, I just had to find them. Just because I don't know or understand something doesn't mean I can't know or understand it. Just because I have failed in relationships before, doesn't mean I can't learn how to succeed moving forward. And just because I haven't loved well in the past doesn't mean I can't learn to love better in the present. While God understands and wants us to know who and where we are in relation to Him and others, this doesn't mean He wants us to remain who and where we are. He loves us much too much to leave us there, and His ultimate desire for us is "to be conformed to the image of His Son" (Romans 8:29). This means that through an intimate, growing relationship with Him, as His apprentices, we can learn to love more like Him and His Son, Jesus. And as we learn, who we are at our core changes, and the natural outflow of how we conduct ourselves within relationships will be one of loving more like Jesus does and not trying so hard to do the right thing.

How?

So how do we love God with all our hearts? We seek after this more intimate relationship with Him. Seeking to find the answers to why we think and feel the way we do, looking for new ideas for how to do life and love, continually looking at Jesus, then looking back at ourselves. Not as a means to shame us, but as a way to look into those mirrors so we can see when we are or aren't doing something in a loving way. Sometimes we do things right. Sometimes we do things wrong. The mirrors show us both. When we do something right, God wants us to know He is so proud of us. When we do something wrong, He wants us to know He loves us unconditionally and how to learn to do it better. Isn't this how good masters teach their apprentices, not solely or primarily by administering consequences? This method only brings shame, guilt, and fear; and it does little to teach us how to do something right, just that there is a price to pay if we do it wrong.

So many of us have been taught this method, even in our relationships with God. And quite honestly, because of our self-focused agendas, it's often the only way to get our attention. But

He isn't a heavy-handed taskmaster who seeks to destroy us for missing the mark. He is a kind, loving teacher, who longs for His students to learn; and He is so proud of them when they act and think in ways that resemble His Son. He is patient and willing to teach and administer appropriate correction for the good of His students. How do we love God with all our hearts? We get to know Him. And as we learn who He really is and how powerful, righteous, and loving He is, while longing to nurture and protect us with all He is, our hearts, even with all their weaknesses, turn toward Him. We begin to understand that not only can He meet all our hearts' longings, but He also desperately wants to do so. But He must do so within the confines of what is true, right, and best—not just seeking to fulfill our selfish needs and desires. We have a propensity to do enough of that ourselves by looking in this world to meet them.

Love Them Big Macs!

I often use an example of my love for McDonald's Big Macs as an example. Now please understand that I have done a lot of hard, inner work dealing with how my attachments to food have been one of the ways I have tried to meet particular needs for myself. So by my using this example, please know that I work hard to be keenly aware of when I am feeding on Big Macs (or anything else) to fill an inner need that belongs to God and when I have one just to enjoy it. This is so much more effective in managing the inner cravings than behavior management and just trying to tell myself no all the time.

I had to be honest with myself at one point in my life. God held this mirror up to me in the form of a Big Mac, so to speak. It was as if He were saying to me, "Look at yourself. Look at how you are stuffing yourself with all that food in an effort to try to satisfy your soul." I learned that food had physiological effects based on when I ate certain things or when I ate a lot of anything; my brain secreted certain chemicals that made me feel satisfied. I became my own drug factory. God let me know He wanted to be the one to meet these deeper needs in my soul. He spoke to my mind and helped me to understand that when I wanted a Big Mac bad enough, I certainly did what it took to get it. I went after it according to how badly I wanted it. It was much the same with alcohol in my younger years. I also used sports to meet a need to feel valued. I learned in each of these areas that I was using the things of this world to meet deeper needs I didn't know how to let God meet. Even though these things in and of themselves were not bad, they had become my idols. He asked my mind, "How badly do you want Me? I have watched you, and I have seen how you have the ability to go after those things you believe will satisfy you, if only for a while. Now it's time for you to go after those things I have to offer, to drink from the fountain that satisfies."

I'm still on the journey of learning to manage worldly things for what their real value to my soul is, because the truth is, all those things satisfied temporarily, but they left me wanting and needing more, which became bondage. I learned that my soul was hungry for a deeper need and that, with Satan's help, it manipulated my mind into thinking I needed food, alcohol, or whatever. And it was causing me unrest until I acted on its desire to have its needs met. I didn't realize at the time what it really needed, nor did I know how to go about getting it met in the proper, healthy way. There is also the idea of learning how to receive love. That's because I didn't always feel that I got the love my soul thought it needed. There was also some learning that needed to happen on how to receive perfect love from a God who loves me unconditionally first and then from those people and things He has placed in my life to make up the difference in how I don't know how to receive from Him.

Natural Love

For me, loving God has started becoming so much more natural as I have spent time with Him and have learned that He has always been pursuing me to make me more like Jesus. While I still don't know how to love Him perfectly, I can return a more natural love, not one that needs all the effort I used to have to put in while trying to obey Him. It is becoming more from the heart (phileo). But in the beginning, it was more from filling my mind with new ideas about Him and seeking after the right things His way, doing and thinking things for the good of my relationship with Him and others (agape love). When I saw the value of these new ideas in meeting my soul's needs, my soul began selling the old ideas and buying the new ones. Agape love and phileo love worked hand in hand to draw me closer and take baby steps toward learning to love like Jesus Christ.

In John 14:15 (NASB), Jesus said, "If you love me, you will keep my commandments." The basis for obedience must be based on love, or it is just a dictatorship. The opposite of this verse would be, "If you don't love me, you will not keep my commandments." Now that's a sobering statement, seeing as how we have all not kept them at times. There's another mirror for us. If I disobey His commandments, this behavior must show me that I'm not loving Him properly. Ouch!

What's God's Love Language?

Have you ever read *The Five Love Languages* by Gary Chapman?[5] It gives some great ideas about how others feel love differently, using terms like "words of affirmation," "acts of service," "receiving gifts," "physical touch," and "quality time." Have you

---

[5] Gary Chapman (1995). The Five Love Languages: How to Express Heartfelt Commitment to Your Mate. Northfield Publishing. ISBN 978-1881273158.

ever spent the time to consider what God's love language is? In what ways can you think or act that would show Him how much you love Him? I believe He gives us a pretty good idea from John 14:15. "If you Love me, you will keep my commandments." That's the reason for the title of this book. I hope we can all agree that because we haven't always kept His commandments, we haven't always loved Him appropriately. Shouldn't we be looking for ways to love Him appropriately? Have you ever asked Him what His love language is and how you can make Him feel loved better? Try it. He just might let you know. But when He does, don't try to make a law or rule out of it. Make it a relational matter.

For me personally:

- If I love Him, I will ... believe that He feels more love from me when I am more aware of His presence throughout the day. I believe this because I know it works for my wife when she knows I have been thinking about her. And He placed this relational side of Himself in her.
- If I love Him, I will ... admit that my way isn't best and that I am willing to seek His ways by studying the ideas He has left us in the Bible.
- If I love Him, I will ... hang out with His people, where I can give and receive from those He is working through to build His kingdom and display as the body of Christ in this world.
- If I love Him, I will ... spend the time to process His ideas, take what He has done for me, and pass it on to others.
- If I love Him, I will ... take the time to disconnect from the cares of this world long enough to be able to hear Him speak, and listen to specific ideas He wants me to know through prayer and fasting.
- If I love Him, I will ... fast from something that is important to my soul's needs long enough to allow my

soul's cravings to try to engage my mind in looking in the right place to satisfy my needs. I will let those cravings be an instant reminder of how my God wants to meet those needs in me and turn my focus back to Him.

- In the process of fasting, as those cravings increase because I am saying no to them and yes to my Father, I am reminded of these things almost constantly because the cravings are so strong. But as I seek after and allow God to meet these needs, the cravings decrease because I am meeting the needs in the proper place. And the fast has found its purpose in getting the deeper needs of my soul met in my relationship with the Father, Son, and Holy Spirit. I know I need to practice these things on occasion because there's just something inside me that tends to want to go back to doing it my way. And with the periodic practice of depriving my soul of meeting its needs my way and seeking after God to meet them, I can feel the difference in the way I love Him, those around me, and even myself in appropriate ways.

  (There may be times when fasting doesn't have this desired outcome, and our souls are still screaming to satisfy their needs. This is a good time to seek wise counsel to get new ideas in our minds for God to use so we can experience His truths in practical ways. Sometimes we just don't have the right ideas to work with in learning how God works with us. Make sure to confide in a trusted therapist or pastor who has exhibited these truths in his or her life.)

- If I love Him, I will ... look in the mirrors He holds up to me through others or life's circumstances, and I will use them to seek more understanding about my relationships with Him, others, and myself.

- If I love Him, I will ... ponder these new ideas and work to appropriate them in all my relationships.
- If I love Him, I will ... acknowledge my need for Him and tell Him I love Him.
- If I love Him, I will ... take the logs out of my eye, stop judging others for their actions, and try to help them understand that what they are doing isn't good for their relationship with God, others, or themselves.
- If I love Him, I will ... learn how to love from Him and practice that love as He provides opportunities to love appropriately.
- If I love Him, I will ... seek to love my wife, family, and those around me in ways that show the unselfish love of Jesus Christ and thankfulness for what He has provided.
- If I love Him, I will ... place proper boundaries in my life to tend to the relationships He has placed in my life, keeping my mind, in as much as I know how, from wandering in ways that would be self-seeking. I will continue to learn and grow from seeking Him, studying, and listening to others around me.
- If I love Him, I will ... practice trusting Him when my fears are kicking in—not necessarily always overcoming the fear but sometimes just "doing it afraid" as I trust His presence, ultimate authority, and direction for my life.
- If I love Him, I will ... allow the learning and practice of agape love to stir the phileo love in my heart for Him and others.
- If I love Him, I will ... pray that He will know it by my thoughts, actions, and responses.

Please take the time to have this conversation with God on what His love language is and how you might be able to make Him feel more loved. He is longing for it.

Others

This category of relationships is vast and must come with prioritization. I doubt I could write a book that contained all the variations and examples of relationships with those around us, but here are some of my ideas.

In understanding this second greatest commandment of loving others as ourselves, we must understand that there will be times when being loving to one may seem unloving to another. This is why it's so important to spend time thinking about prioritization of love. I believe it's evident that when we need to choose between appropriate love of more than one, God is the first and foremost thought in the process. In other words, how are my thoughts or actions showing my love for God? Hopefully, you won't be faced with many situations where you will need to choose who feels loved by your actions, but you should spend some time thinking about it just in case or have a list ready if and when it happens. Your list may look different or be in a different order than mine, but for me—and no list is perfect—the prioritization would look something like this:

1. God
2. My spouse
3. My family I have with my spouse (children, adopted children, blended family)
4. My birth family, adoptive family (I was adopted into), or family by marriage
5. My church family
6. My friends
7. My coworkers
8. My community
9. Self
    *   There is another priority that should be considered in this process, but I didn't assign it a number because it

will be different for everyone, and quite frankly for me, all the above are included in the process of thinking about it. And that is our country or nation. To have put it on the list would have been difficult because no matter where I put it, I would have put it before or after others, and there are those who have served and/or died for our country, and I couldn't find a comfortable number to assign to it. So let's just understand that all the above are the reasons we pray and fight for our country.

- Another one I wasn't certain of where to prioritize it, because it can change so easily, is learning how to love our enemies appropriately. This is something God desires for us to learn, and He can place it anywhere on this list if He has put us in a position to be His witnesses. But this must be done with much prayer and seeking since it would be difficult to know when to love our enemy by placing him or her in priority above any on our list if doing so made anyone on our list feel unloved. Missionaries, I am sure, have to deal with some of this issue as they place the needs of those they are trying to reach above others in their world. So in any prioritizing, it's essential to seek Godly wisdom and understanding.

Please take the time to prioritize relationships in your life. The list doesn't have to look like mine. But I believe it must line up in the order of loving God, others, and self. A significant thing to remember is that behaviors like abuse can drastically change this priority list. If our spouses were somehow abusing our children, then the priority of loving our children and doing what is best for them would take precedence over our spouses. And actually what would be best for our spouses is to not let them continue in their abuse and seek help, even if the situation warranted turning them into the authorities. Remember, agape love tries to do what is best for all concerned. It is never best to allow someone trapped in abusive behavior, either the abuser or the abused, to continue in the abuse.

So let's take a closer look at how love should look as we learn from the Master how to apply it to other relationships.

My Spouse

I think one of the most difficult lessons for us to learn is how to prioritize agape love when it concerns our spouses and natural-born family members. Many times we feel like we are caught in the middle when there is a choice to make concerning whom I should show agape love to when I feel like I have to choose between these two. But God makes it very clear what His intentions are in this matter. Genesis 2:24 says, "That is why a man leaves his father and mother and is united to his wife, and they become one flesh."

I believe it's vitally important for my wife to "feel" like she has a priority over everything in my life except God. In general, she will get those feelings of priority by how I respond to situations that present themselves to prove this fact to her. Now anytime we have this conversation, we need to allow the idea that it's possible that my wife didn't feel like she received the love and priority her soul felt it needed earlier in life, and she may be trying to meet her soul's needs primarily from me. In this case, there would be undue pressure for me to continually prove she is number one or two in my life (after God). If the spouse feels this kind of pressure, it's usually best to confide in a third party like a licensed therapist and/or a respected pastor who can help sort it out, because the two parties may not be able to see clearly enough because of the emotions this issue can stir.

Aside from any struggles caused by a person's past, spouses should know and feel where they stand in this matter. When faced with a circumstance that makes me feel like "I'm caught in the middle," I must first look at how my thoughts or actions show agape love for God, then for my wife, and then for my natural family. This is no doubt a very difficult process at times and will be a product of how we have prepared ourselves for these decisions beforehand. If I have never taken the time to contemplate these things with God and have had some conversations with my wife about how I make her feel, it will be difficult to make the right decisions when I am in the middle of it all. This also doesn't mean I completely ignore how my natural family feels about the circumstance, just that when it comes down to making decisions, what is best for God and my wife or our family must be the first priority. If this causes hurt feelings to my natural family, then it is my responsibility to help them understand the process of my decision in as much of a loving way as I know how. Sometimes we feel like we are in the middle because that is precisely where we are. And rightly so. My natural family and my wife, in many circumstances, may not be able to work through these circumstances properly.

This priority must also extend to all other relationships below God and my spouse. My wife should never be made to feel like I care more about my friends than about her. If she does, then we need to communicate and try to determine whether I am doing things in a way that makes her feel this way or whether I'm just triggering something in her. This is when she would have to be real honest with herself, look in that mirror, and realize that she may be asking me to satisfy needs that aren't entirely my responsibility to fulfill. I know there are some fine lines here that may be hard to discern, but the red flags are the feelings she is experiencing. It is vitally important that, when she has these kinds of emotions, she sits down with me and helps me to understand that when I have done a specific thing, it made her feel in a particular way. Or else how will I ever understand what I can do to change it?

She must also learn to get more in touch with how she is feeling from the offense so she can get better at explaining it. We men weren't made the relational ones; we need a little more explanation in ways we can truly understand the impact of our decisions. When most people, men and women, are communicated with in a way that helps them to realize that their choices have made God or their spouse feel unloved, invaluable, and unconsidered, would be quicker to say this wasn't their intention. And when others come to us to try to help us understand how we made them feel, our first response should never be to defend what we have done. This is a twisting of the proverbial knife, and it says to the offended soul, "Not only did I choose to hurt you, but I will now tell you how I had a good reason to do so." This is where things fly off the rails. Now the issue becomes a mudslinging contest while we try to defend ourselves and win the disagreement.

The first thing we should always do when others are trying to help us understand how we made them feel, is to listen. Try to understand how they are feeling, whether we agree with them or not. We shouldn't try to correct their feelings. We should first acknowledge their hurt, then let them know that hurting them wasn't our intention if we can honestly say that. But we must be honest with ourselves. I have said things to my wife I later said I didn't mean, or I said I didn't mean to hurt her, but at that moment, hurting her to "one-up" her had been exactly what my intentions were. I need to look closely at these things because I have ways of engaging in battle I have learned to be effective with. And when in the circumstance, attacking or withdrawing is certainly a way to engage we have learned to use. Both are equally destructive to a relationship. Attacking just destroys much faster. In these cases, my only option is to be aware of what my intentions truly were, explain my understanding of them, apologize for them, and work hard not to intentionally hurt again. When I deal with the hurt first, I set the stage for better, more caring, communication. And she is more willing to hear what my reasoning was for doing what I did if she believes the intent wasn't to hurt her.

Then we can have adult conversations about our differences without drawing all the battle lines, which only lead to—guess what? Battle. If we are both trying hard to be aware of our own wounds, our own feelings, and how we are engaging in our differences and not making the whole of our relationship about this one issue, then we can usually keep it from spinning out of control. We don't always have to agree on everything. But by truly understanding how the other person feels and what he or she thinks in the matter while listening to understand genuinely, then we set the stage for compromise. We won't and shouldn't always give in or fight until we win. Sometimes we give in, sometimes the other person gives in, and sometimes we work through the issue like loving Christian adults and come to agreements we can both proceed with. When we show this kind of agape love of checking our words and intentions for the damage they are capable of and making willful choices, not to intentionally hurt each other but to listen as well as to be heard, then our hearts are much more inclined to allow phileo love to be part of the process. This example goes for anything we may be putting before our spouse except God, and putting our spouse second to God should be a close second, not a distant second.

Agape love in any relationship between spouses means they are always trying to make willful choices that are best for their relationship with God, with those around them, and with themselves. If I have needs that aren't being met, then I need to get better at helping her understand them while not attacking her for it. First Peter 3:7 (KJV) says, "Likewise, ye husbands, dwell with them according to knowledge, giving honour unto the wife, as unto the weaker vessel."

God once gave me a vision of this weaker vessel when I was

speaking harshly to my wife. He gave me an image in my mind's eye of Him giving me a fragile million-dollar vessel or vase, and then watching it be shattered by my words and attitudes toward her. I know today that I have the capacity to shatter, and I work hard not to do so anymore. I wish I could say I was perfect at it, but she has loved me through it, and I am getting better and better. And I try hard to take the sting out of the offense, not just by apologizing but by helping her to know what I am apologizing for. I believe she has been able to endure the hard times because she sees something better in me and because I try to have the right conversations with her today instead of just attacking her.

Sometimes we have let our relationship go unattended or allowed the harmful or destructive ways of relating go on for so long that we find ourselves in an uphill battle concerning the health of our relationship. Have you ever heard or said the following? "I love them, but I am not in love with them." This is where agape love and phileo love has one of their biggest distinctions between the two. This statement, actually thought out, would say something like this: "I care about them and what happens to them, but I don't have the emotional feelings toward them that I used to." This is when a relationship could be in trouble. There are those, especially from an older generation, who understand the idea of commitment. And when they reach this point, they stay in the relationship because of their commitment. I believe most marriages will go through stages like this, but it isn't the ideal relationship to be in. And while many from that generation have stayed together because of agape love that said, "I am committed to you and will continue to do what is best for you," many of them have never understood how to truly make the relationship better in a way that the heart (phileo love) could re-engage. Nor did many feel comfortable going to see a therapist or pastor for advice on how to make it better.

I have spoken with people who wear their commitment as a badge of honor, all the while wishing they didn't have to live in a relationship of agape love without phileo love. While I am a huge proponent of commitment to a relationship, I don't agree that settling for it that way is good for either one and can be very burdensome. I love the commitment of agape love but also believe that part of its purpose is to hold the relationship together as the two find ways to work through the difficulties in healthy ways, and both learn to do things that will allow for the heart to re-engage in phileo love. There are also many relationships based mainly on phileo love. Love of the heart and emotions has very little lasting commitment of agape love when things get difficult. That's probably one of the reasons the divorce rate is so high. I will make a bold statement here. I believe most relationships start with an emphasis on phileo love. We get married because of how the other person makes us feel and how he or she meets our personal needs. But I believe we stay married because of agape love, always trying to do what is best for the other in spite of how we might feel in the heart. And as I said, this is when we need to recognize that there is something unhealthy taking place in our relationship, engage the agape love of commitment, and begin to learn ways to work through things in a way that will free the heart to feel safe to love (phileo) again.

I believe God meant for intimate relationships to contain both agape and phileo love. But I also believe He knows how our hearts work and that phileo love can wax and wane as it goes through the process of mingling one's hopes, dreams, thoughts, and ideas with another. But He wants to teach us that agape love is how we stay committed to relationships while the heart vacillates. This is how He has remained committed to loving us. While we have all missed the mark (sinned) in our relationship with Him, He has remained committed to us, doing what is best for us, even though we may hurt His heart by our unloving thoughts or deeds. He always stands ready with forgiveness, but His intention isn't solely to forgive but to teach how and why we have and continue to miss the mark (sin) so we can change our minds (repent) and move toward more loving thoughts and actions in our relationship with Him. And from there, we can learn to be in healthier, more appropriate relationships with those around us, even with ourselves.

When it comes to my relationship with my wife:

- If I love her, I will … seek after God with more tenacity than I have ever sought after food or anything else I pursued to meet the needs of my soul, and to learn to love her better.
- If I love her, I will … always try to understand how my thoughts and actions would or are making her feel, and I will always try to do what is best for her. This in itself will take my entire lifetime to learn, but if I love her … I will.
- If I love her, I will … listen to her when she tells me that I have done something to hurt her or have done something that isn't good for her. I will seek to understand first and then to be understood. I will try to understand how she is feeling from her perspective, not mine (empathy).
- If I love her, I will … understand the precious vase God has given me and be ever so careful not to damage it.
- If I love her, I will … take care of myself physically, emotionally, and spiritually. I will seek to be there for her when needed in any of these areas.
- If I love her, I will … be honest with her in a loving way when I see something in her that isn't good for her relationship with God, others, or herself (truth in love).
- If I love her, I will … place proper boundaries in my life to manage those temptations that seem to be inherent in me as a man. I won't just say no in the situation that

tempts me, but I will try to place boundaries in a way that prevents me from being in that situation to begin with and will keep my mind and actions as clean as possible, even when no one else is there to see them, because I'm always in the presence of my Lord.

- If I love her, I will ... continue to seek and study who I am and why I do what I do so I can look into those mirrors, make needed changes, and place proper boundaries as my understanding grows.

- If I love her, I will ... try to see past her responses to me and seek to understand where I may be prompting those responses or touching a wound. If I come to realize I am touching a wound, then I need to find appropriate ways to try to help her heal and not just expect her to change for my good. I must understand that loving her properly also means not turning my head, walking on eggshells, or hoping the situation will get better but learning how to have the right, loving conversations with her and genuinely seeking what is best for her, even if I have to be firm at times. This one will depend on my relationship with God as He leads me into actions of truth and love. It greatly helps to have an accountability partner or counselor with whom to walk through the situation, since our emotions can often cloud our intentions.

- If I love her, I will ... love her with an agape love learned from my relationship with Jesus Christ. And even when my heart isn't engaged, I will always engage my mind and will to do what is best for her until my heart re-engages. And I will work to find ways to nurture both my agape and phileo love for her.

- If I love her, I will ... pray that she will know my love by my actions and responses.

My Family I Have Made with My Spouse

In the same context as our spouses feeling like they are above everything but God concerning our choices, our families should be made to feel the same way after God and our spouses. Please remember that in our formative years, our souls gain their understanding of how their basic human needs are being met. This starts with our family structure. Regardless of intentions, our souls will learn how loved, and valuable they are. How safe and secure they are. And how much power and control they have over their ability to maneuver through life. When we aren't taught the truth about these matters as God would have us learn them, then we believe whatever lies have been placed in us about any of these needs. And this will set the stage for how we will seek these things, either from God or from the world later in life. These will result in a state of health or being wounded that we bring into all our relationships, especially the more intimate ones. It's like that bottle of water. When pressure was put on it, what came out? Water. Why? Because that is what was put in it; like it or not, this is how it works.

So parents, be very mindful of what you are pouring into your children or what you see others pouring into them. This is what will be in them and what they will have to operate from when they get older. Work hard to understand God's ideas of how to love appropriately in all your relationships so you can pass these things on to your children. Then you can quite possibly save them from a whole lot of pain and prevent someone else from needing to pour better things into them, so when the pressure comes, anything unhealthy you poured into them won't come out.

Sometimes when one spouse is doing things the other spouse believes is out of order in prioritizing the family, it is the right and responsibility of the other spouse to help the spouse understand what he or she is doing. This may require counseling with a therapist or pastor to help the spouse be able to present it in a way that is understood and not just coming at the other spouse in a way that would make him or her feel attacked. Truth in love must always guide these interactions, helping them to understand the truth about what their actions are doing to the family in a way that says, "I love you, and I love our family, and this is what I perceive is happening. Let's talk it through in a way that shows this love for each other and our family."

Men, if your wife comes to you to have a conversation, please remember to listen first to try to understand what she is telling you. If she isn't the best at communicating and is attacking or withdrawing, then know that there is another issue behind it, and you need to try having the right conversation to get what she is trying to convey. Some just aren't good at communicating their feelings and frustrations to you, and learned responses may be what you are seeing. Be patient since she is trying to help you understand something for the good of the family. Examine what she is saying. Look in the mirror to see whether something she is saying is true and continue respectful conversations if you disagree with something. Remember that God has made her the relational one. And if you are doing something that is harmful to the relationship, you should listen with the intent to try to understand what she is telling you, even if you have to keep asking questions until you understand what she is saying. Then you can proceed to present your case in the matter. If you are both trying to love God, each other, and your family appropriately, you will work in a better direction. Never be too prideful to ask for help if needed for the benefit of all concerned.

There are also times of "tough love." If you find yourself in a situation with children or family members and have done all you can to try to help them yet their behavior hasn't changed, then sometimes doing what is best for them (agape love) is not enabling them in their behavior any longer. I have found that this step is especially difficult for women since they are so engaged from the heart (phileo love) that they sometimes need help to see that their phileo love is enabling their child's bad behavior. Agape love would dictate a different response to them because it is what is best for them. This isn't to say that men are experts at agape love, just usually not as in touch with the phileo aspect of their relationships as women usually are. There is a lot of information one can find on walking through this "tough love," and it is beyond the scope of this book.

For me personally:

- If I love my family, I will ... seek to find a deeper understanding of who God is, what He has done for us, and how He teaches us to love each other. I cannot pass on what I don't have. And just because I don't have it now doesn't mean I can't learn it and pass it on no matter what age I am. Our children, small and tall, are always in learning mode and will learn from us as we live life.
- If I love my family, I will ... seek to learn how to love my wife in a way that shows her and the world around us that I am striving to do what is best for her so I may lead by example in how to love in an intimate and Godly way. Then my children will know how to do the same when the time comes.
- If I love my family, I will ... find ways to help them understand that God is number one, and my wife is number two; this will hold true unless she has placed them in physical or emotional danger. They must never be allowed to feel like they can cause division between us.
- If I love my family, I will ... always try to do what is best for them, making the necessary sacrifices in my life that may place questions in their minds about how

much I love them and being ready with a truth-in-love explanation if they don't understand my decision.

- If I love my family, I will ... discipline in a way that is always considering what is best for them, not from the emotions they have triggered in me. This again is a learning and growing process. If I make a mistake in parenting, I will go to them if appropriate, apologize for my mistake, and explain how I will try to better love them in the future.
- If I love my family, I will ... try always to make them feel like they come before everything except God and my wife. And I will help them to understand why that priority must be so.
- If I love my family, I will ... pray that they will know my love by my actions and responses.

My Birth Family or Adoptive Family

Let there be no question. Only God, spouse and immediate family should come before our natural or adoptive family. As imperfect as they may have been, this is who we are. Some of who we are needs to change, but our roots should never be forgotten (generally speaking). I know there are circumstances in which our natural or adoptive families are so hurtful to either us or our new families that firm boundaries or even separation may need to take place. But for most of us, staying close is a big part of how we tend to our souls' needs going forward, while we work hard at trying to understand the things poured into us that weren't so healthy and need to be changed. I work equally as hard trying to understand the healthy things that were poured into me so I can build on the good and right things that are also part of who I am at the core. It is good to understand these things about myself, so I can hone them and allow God to use them for Kingdom purposes.

While I am the first to admit I have some wounds from my formation, I will also be the first to admit there are some great attributes that were given to me about how to care for and nurture others that came from my roots as a child and how to look outside of myself for the good of others. And I gained an understanding that there is a God who created and loved us enough to pursue us. I will forever be grateful for the good, right, and true things my family placed in me. And I work hard to be honest about the not-so-good things or untruths that were placed in me. This includes understanding and believing that my parents loved me and did the best they knew how to do, letting God change negatives into positives, never blaming or pointing fingers at the past, and being ever grateful and mindful of the good.

For me personally:

- If I love my birth family, I will ... spend time understanding all the good attributes they passed on to me so I can hone them and pass on this legacy to my family.
- If I love my birth family, I will ... be honest about the not-so-good things that were passed on to me, take personal responsibility for them, and seek to change them, so they aren't passed on to future generations. If possible, I will sit down with my family and discuss these things, not as a family criticism but in a way that says, "I love my family and want us to be the best we can be." Treading lightly and prayerfully down this road of "truth in love," rules the day here.
- If I love my birth family, I will ... make efforts to let them know that even though I must prioritize my new family, they are right there with me, and I haven't forgotten or forsaken where I come from and who brought me here.
- If I love my birth family, I will ... pray that they will know my love by my actions and responses.

My Church Family

I know it may be difficult to completely identify what we would term as our "church family." It can mean all those who profess a belief in Christ, those believers in my life, or those who attend the same church I do. So while there is commonness among all these, I will focus my conversation on those who attend the same church. These are the ones I will be in the most contact with, worshipping with regularly and living the Christian life with. I think sometimes we don't put enough thought into how we are showing the body of Christ our love, and often we stay focused on how they make us feel loved.

Former president John F. Kennedy said, "My fellow Americans, ask not what your country can do for you, ask what you can do for your country." This statement would bode well in the church setting. Although I understand that there are those coming to a church who still are in need of receiving what the church has to offer, there are many who should be growing to the point of understanding their primary role as servants and everything in between.

Here is an analogy for consideration. If we look at our church family as analogous to our personal family, we will see that some things play out in like manner. When we are born into our personal family, we are welcomed into the family, not asked to contribute anything to the well-being of the family, and we are able to enjoy the fruits of the family labor. In much the same way, when new believers come into the church family, I believe they can come in with no expectations put on them and enjoy the fruits of the church family. As children grow, they start learning to do some basic tasks that help the family structure. And as they grow in stature, knowledge, and wisdom, they take on more meaningful duties to aid in the well-being of the family. So it is with coming into a church family.

At some point, we begin by learning to contribute in

whatever ways we are learning to do so. And as we grow, we learn more ways to contribute to the family structure. There is also a time when we have come to a place where we are beginning to support our own needs yet still living at home. At some point in the family relationship, we start to understand that the family needs our help in monetary ways as well as physical ones. So at some point, we begin to contribute financially to the good of the family, so we aren't just using them to meet our needs but are willing to share with them what we have been given as well. In the church, there comes the point when we should want to contribute to the financial well-being of the church because we love our church family and want to do what is best for them, not just because someone said we are supposed to tithe.

Remember that sin means missing the mark. At some point, we are missing the mark in our relationship with our church family if we don't contribute our part to the good of our church family. If I want to have agape love for my church family, I will consider how to love them back. This section is on the church family. There are those ideas of loving God back through serving and participating financially. And not doing so at some point would have to be considered missing the mark in our relationship with God and our church family. Yes, at some point, it would be called sin by these standards—not by the standard of law breaking but by the standard of not loving appropriately.

For me personally:

- If I love my church family, I will ... seek to grow in my relationship with Jesus Christ in a manner that shows my love for Him and the Father. And I will do my best to live by the example of that love.
- If I love my church family, I will ... spend time thinking about where I am in the family process so I might do my best to show them my love by how I understand I

should be serving and contributing at this point in my Christian and church family growth.

- If I love my church family, I will ... show my love for them by participating in family gatherings and praying for them on a regular basis.
- If I love my church family, I will ... Learn when and where I can pass lessons learned on to others who are wanting to grow, even mentoring if God has placed the opportunity.
- If I love my church family, I will ... pray that they will know my love by my actions and responses.

My Friends

Friendships are where phileo love really come into play because we generally have friends we have heart feelings for. If we don't really care for someone for whatever reason, we usually aren't very close friends with him or her. This is where many find it very difficult sometimes to also show agape love to their friends. Many times, we are unwilling to do or say what is best for them because we don't want to risk losing their friendship. But agape love dictates that if it's best for them to have a particular conversation, then we should have agape love for them and pray that our friendship will be sustained or even grow through it. If you genuinely have agape love for your friends and see them doing something that isn't good for their relationship with God, those around them, or themselves, then that love should compel you to try to have some kind of conversation with them. There may even be circumstances that dictate a separation of the friendship for their benefit, so you aren't condoning their actions if they are harmful.

We must also be cautious about the influences we allow in our lives and those we allow to influence our families. Remember that spouse and family are a higher priority than friends, and if a situation comes when you must prioritize, spouse and family must come first. This structure should be followed with an explanation to friends of why you felt like you had to make a choice and were compelled to choose family. If this has been explained well, I find it hard to believe that most wouldn't understand. Are you selecting friends who are healthy for your relationship with God, your spouse, your family, and so forth? Are you a friend who is healthy for your friend's relationships with God, spouses, family, and so forth?

For me personally:

- If I love my friends, I will … seek after God with all my heart so I can be an example for them and support their relationships with Him.
- If I love my friends, I will … hold myself accountable to them and listen if they are trying to tell me something they see in me that isn't healthy.
- If I love my friends, I will … be honest with them if I see something in them that is harmful to their relationship with God, others, or themselves. This is truth in love.
- If I love my friends, I will … pray that they will know this love by my actions and responses.

Coworkers

In trying to show agape love to our coworkers, there are different dynamics to be considered. Usually, in a work environment, there runs a gamut of personalities, belief systems, ethics, and life experiences. For me as a Christian, one of the ways I have found to do what is best for my coworkers is to be as true to my faith as I know how to be. This means walking the walk I profess and doing my best not to be hypocritical. Many in the workplace weren't exposed to the same type of faith training I had. They may come from different faith systems or have no faith-based system at all. Trying to convince them that I am right and that they have it wrong will only set them on the defense and cause them not to want to hear what I have to say. As in all relationships, they must first believe that I care about them before they are willing to listen to me.

The truth is, many Christians are more concerned about being right than about loving the person they are speaking to. We must be grounded enough in our belief system to be able to hear what others believe. This sets the stage for an honest conversation to follow. When others have strong feelings about their beliefs and those are different from ours, we shouldn't try to take away their right to believe what they believe. We should listen to what they believe and then do our best to explain why our belief is worth considering. And never forget, we have the Holy Spirit to help and guide us through these conversations, and it's never our place to try to bully someone into believing our way. I have personally witnessed pastors who operated in this manner, and I am confident they were operating from their own ideas and not God's in those moments. I am sure I have done the same thing at times because I'm just as capable; thus, there is the need to be ever aware of how I am being perceived so the message isn't skewed by my own dysfunctional behaviors.

As we seek to live, feel, and love like Christ would in any situation, I believe who we are and who we are becoming should allow us to tend to relationships with coworkers in most cases. These relationships can be very superficial, or they can lead to lifetime friendships and bonds. After coming from the workforce to become a pastor, I have had the privilege of marrying and performing memorial services for many friends. I can only hope and pray that most of them would testify to how I acted in those work relationships. Of course, that was a growing process as well, so the further we go back, the less likely I would have been to understand how to relate to them properly. As I said in an earlier chapter, I pray that anyone I hurt or offended in my lack of knowing how to live differently would forgive me and believe that I am trying my best to seek God in a way that continues to change those things in me that can hurt others. I know I will be after that one for the rest of my life.

Coworkers also have a high capacity to offend us. Does this mean that because we have been offended, we have the right to return the offense? Certainly not. This can be one of the most significant opportunities to show agape love. While we have the right and, I would argue, the responsibility to go to others and help them understand how they have made us feel, we certainly shouldn't return evil for evil, even if they don't respond favorably to our conversation, and if the offense is severe enough, it may be in the best interest of my other coworkers, my family, and me to seek help from the organization we work for to help correct the situation. For the most part, if we work hard, treat others with respect, and live what we profess, most work relationships will be healthy. For those who don't play well with others, there are usually organizational resources to help. I am sure there are some horror stories that don't fit this description, but we must always remember as Christians whom we represent.

For me personally:

- If I love my coworkers, I will … try to live my faith by example. This comes by being a living testimony of my faith so when they need God with skin, they know where to go.
- If I love my coworkers, I will … pray that they will know this love by my actions and responses.

My Community

At the writing of this book, I had recently retired as a pastor. At the time, I lived over thirty miles away from the church I had the privilege of serving. Now understand that my wife and I grew up in the community where our church was, and we attended the church for nearly a dozen years before we moved to another community to live with her mother after her husband went home to Jesus. So even though we lived in another community, it wasn't hard to stay connected, even though we didn't live there. However, when I retired to help the changing needs of our family, we made a heart-wrenching decision to find a church in our new community. We had been living there for about sixteen years and knew very few in our community because we were so connected to another community. We wanted to learn to worship with those who are close to where we lived, shopped, and bought fuel.

After much searching, we found a local community of believers that most resembled the Kingdom. And on the day I wrote these words, we committed to join a new church family. This was a bittersweet day in our lives as God leads us into another chapter. Our hearts will always remember our previous church family since we were with them for twenty-five years. Our lives were changed there. We learned how to commit to God and others there. And I owe a debt of gratitude to the pastor, Fred Young, who provided a safe environment for change. It is because of the opportunities he offered me, that allowed me to change as much from the day he commissioned me to be a pastor to who I am today, as from the day God pulled me off a bar stool and moved me toward being a pastor. Thank you, Fred Young, and East Side Baptist Church for being my church family for so long, helping me, and providing an environment for me to learn how to love God and others as myself. You will always be part of who I am and what others might receive from me through our Lord.

So I am endeavoring to learn how to take what I have learned from previous relationships concerning church family and move into a new church family and new relationships. There is sadness as we move forward, but it is greatly mixed with excitement as we learn how to love our new community and new brothers and sisters in Christ. My wife and I have deliberate conversations about how we should move forward on this journey. We have joined a small group already and are committed to volunteering in areas that will help us get to know our new family faster. We are looking forward to how God will use us to help those in our new community.

They have already helped us by allowing a new safe place for us to worship, learn and grow. In the short time we have been on this new journey in our new community, we have met more people from our community than we did during the previous sixteen years. We are starting to see people we know while shopping at the store, getting fuel, or going out to eat. We hope this interaction will enhance our love for our new town (after sixteen years), and we look forward to how God will use us here. I personally know some very strong Christians who are very involved in various ways in their communities, including sports programs, community events, politics, community goodwill, and various ways of helping the community to improve and be healthy.

I believe God would have us to be involved in our communities in ways that say, "This is who we are as Christians." Then we can be an example of both agape and phileo love in this world. This also presents opportunities to tell people about the one who saved and changed our lives.

For me personally:

- If I love my community, I will ... seek to conform to the image of Jesus Christ in a way that allows me to be a living testimony of His love and goodness.
- If I love my community, I will ... engage in ways that say I care about people, and maybe from appropriate relationships; I might have the opportunity to share my

faith in a way that would cause others to consider this God who lives in me.

* If I love my community, I will ... pray that others see this love in my actions and responses to them.

Self

Here is a principle of God and life I had to learn the hard way. In many of my studies, I heard scripture quoted by respected teachers who taught me I should hate myself. And as I grew, I was perplexed by the second greatest commandment telling me to "love others as myself." So I was supposed to hate others too? I will save you the time of laying out what others teach on this subject only because what I am about to teach is probably different from what most teach anyway. Yes, this is always an area of caution—coming to a conclusion that doesn't agree with the norm. But I'm pretty confident that what I have to say is of immense value and is backed up by what I believe God would have us believe about loving ourselves appropriately.

In my opinion, the reason this topic is so controversial and difficult to dissect is that most authors I have read deal only with the subject from an English translation of the word *love*. I hope you have a better feel for the subject of this book since the word *love* is expressed in more than one way in the original Greek. The whole reason I decided to write this book was so others would come to a deeper understanding of what love is in the different forms expressed in scripture and life. So here we will examine how the principles of agape and phileo love play out in loving ourselves.

Please remember that when God gave us a new idea for all scripture to come into the context of loving God with all our hearts, souls, and minds (and loving others as ourselves), He used the Greek word *agape*, making willful choices for the good of Him and others, versus phileo, a love of the emotions.

Without understanding how these two differ from each other and play out in our relationships, we cannot attain a good understanding of what love is in the context of any relationship, let alone a relationship with ourselves.

I want to share a scripture you have probably heard in various ways of translation. Here is my version within the context of this book's teachings. John 21:15–17 says,

> When they had finished eating, Jesus said to Simon Peter, "Simon son of John, do you love me more than these?"
>
> "Yes, Lord," he said, "you know that I love you."
>
> Jesus said, "Feed my lambs."
>
> Again Jesus said, "Simon son of John, do you love me?"
>
> He answered, "Yes, Lord, you know that I love you."
>
> Jesus said, "Take care of my sheep."
>
> The third time he said to him, "Simon son of John, do you love me?"
>
> Peter was hurt because Jesus asked him the third time, "Do you love me?" He said, "Lord, you know all things; you know that I love you."

There is more than one use of the English word for *love* used here. Listen to how I believe this story goes. Jesus asked Peter three times whether he loved Him. And here is how the conversation unfolded in the Greek language:

The First Ask:

- Jesus:
  o "Simon son of John, do you love me more than these?"

- Literally, do you have *agapas* for me? *Agapas* is a form of the word *agapao*. Notice the same root word as in *agape*?
- Peter's answer:
    o "You know that I love you."
        - Literally, you know that I have *philo* for you.
            - *Philo* is a form of the word *phileo*.
- My interpretation:
    o Jesus literally asked Peter, "Do you have agape love for Me? Have you made a willful decision to love Me and do what is in My best interest?"
    o Peter basically answered by saying, "You know that I love [*philo*] you with all my heart."
        - That is not what Jesus asked him.

So Jesus asked him again, "Simon son of John, do you love me more than these?"

    o Again, He used the agape form of love. "Have you made a willful decision to love Me and do what is in My best interest over these others?"
    o Again, Peter answered, "You know that I love [*philo*] you with all my heart."
        - Again, that's not what Jesus asked.
- Here's the twist:
    o For the third time when Jesus asked Peter, He changed His word to the one Peter had been using.
        - "Do you have *phileis* for me?" *Phileis* is another form of the word *phileo*. He had asked him twice whether he had agape love for Him. "Have you made a willful decision to love Me and do what is in my best interest?" And both times Peter answered with a phileo answer. "I love you with all of my heart." The third time Jesus questioned

whether he really loved Him with all his heart. This is shown in the following sentence: "Peter was hurt because Jesus asked him the third time, 'Do you love me?'"

- So the conversation went more like this:
  - o "Peter, have you made a willful decision to love Me and do what is in My best interest?" Peter answered, "Lord, You know I love You with all my heart." Jesus asked him again, "Peter, have You made a willful decision to love Me and do what is in My best interest?" Peter answered, "Lord, You know that I love You with all my heart." Jesus asked him a third time, "Peter, do you love Me with all of your heart?" Peter was hurt because Jesus had asked him the third time, "Do you love Me with all your heart?" He said, "Lord, You know all things. You know that I love You with all of my heart."

Peter did love Jesus with all his heart as he knew it. But he also proved that he had not made a willful decision to love Him and do what was in His best interest when he denied knowing Him later. Remember, in an earlier chapter I said Jesus was the master of holding up a mirror to show us, us. This is precisely what He did with Peter. He taught Peter that he needed to make a willful choice to love and do what was best and right no matter what. And He even made him look at the phileo love he thought he had for Jesus. Have you ever had others tell you that they loved you with all their hearts, only for them to make willful choices that were unloving to you? This happens all the time in relationships. Peter moved on from here to become one of the boldest apostles, even willing to die for what he believed about Jesus.

I walk through this example in a section about loving ourselves for a reason. It is a perfect example of how we should love with both agape and phileo love. I think by now you have a pretty good idea of how agape and phileo love should look in your relationship with God and others. Now let's look closer at how they should look in your relationship with yourself.

Agape and Phileo Concerning Self

If in my understanding of love for myself I use the idea of phileo love, an emotional love for myself, the decisions to follow will usually be to make choices for myself that make me feel good or loved. While there is a healthy emotional love for self, this can also be a recipe for disaster. To seek after the meeting of my basic human needs in this way could be seeking after a hedonistic way of trying to meet these desires. Unfortunately, this is the way the world would teach us to have love for one's self. It also seems to be the way we love ourselves when we are young or immature.

God's primary idea of appropriate love for yourself is one of agape love. Making a willful decision to love yourself in a way that you make choices from your mind to do what is best for your life from how He is teaching you what is best, and not so much about what will make you feel better or more loved. Generally speaking, it is natural for us to seek after those things that would satisfy our basic human needs of power and control, love and esteem, security and survival. This is the human nature God wants to change into a nature that is more aligned with His ideas of what is good for our relationship with Him, others, and ourselves. Our human nature to miss the mark in these relationships is precisely what He is trying to convert to a nature that hits the mark in these relationships. As we grow in Christ and in His knowledge and understanding of what agape love is, we begin to make better long-term decisions for ourselves and not as many that satisfy temporarily but have negative consequences in the long term.

Here is a scripture that hits home in the area of loving ourselves inappropriately. John 12:25 says, "Anyone who loves their life will lose it, while anyone who hates their life in this world will keep it for eternal life."

This mention of the word *love* is a form of phileo. A good understanding of this would translate to, "Anyone who has a heart for themselves will lose his or her life." *Hate* was translated from a word *miseo*, which carries the idea of renouncing one choice in favor of another or the elevation of one moral idea over another, not the typical sense of hate as we think of it. The whole concept is a warning about having a heart for oneself over the Godly idea of agape love, which is making willful choices to love God and others as ourselves.

So in prioritizing how we show love, we can see that we should put others before ourselves, and we should always be making willful choices that are in line with how we appropriately love God and others as well as ourselves.

For me personally:

- If I love myself, I will ... always seek to know and understand my God, the one who died for me, Jesus Christ, and the one who was given to me, the Holy Spirit, in ways that will increase my experience with them to change who I am at the core and learn how to love them back for what they have done for me.
- If I love myself, I will ... ask God to show me who I truly am at the core, why I am that way, and in what ways I can receive ideas from Him that would mature me in this school of love. And from this, I would learn how to speak to that little boy in me and help him to understand how much he is loved, how valuable he is, how safe and secure he is, and how he has the power to make right and Godly decisions for himself and those around him. And when I tell him no, it is for his best

good, but I will always try to show him the proper things to say yes to instead.

- If I love myself, I will ... pray that I will understand this love by the change I see in learning to love God and others appropriately, and I will do my part to make a difference in this world by learning from the Master.

CHAPTER 15

Maturing Love

I pray that this book has set the stage for learning how to love from the mind (agape) and not just from the heart (phileo). A maturing love that resembles that of our creator is both from the heart and emotions, and from the mind and will. But mature Christian love will be primarily governed by agape love. That love says I will do my best to do what is best for my relationships with God, others, and myself. I pray this will become a goal for each of us. Setting goals always keeps our eyes on the purpose and keeps hope alive.

My goal in life is to someday graduate from this school of Jesus and love, and be in the physical presence of my God and the Lord Jesus Christ. This goal often helps me when life happens in ways that cause pain in the present. My goal in learning how to love like Christ keeps me evaluating and learning when I don't do so well but keeps me pressing toward the goal. Maturing isn't just a matter of aging but of learning, growing, and sharing what we have learned with others. Since I have watched the aging process take place in others many times now, I have come to understand the aging process as a refining of the soul and a stripping away of the things in the world we have turned to, to meet our basic human needs. If we live long enough, we will begin to change the emphasis from these things, to those relationships around us. The last things to be stripped away, like health and cognitive processing, will give way to intimacy with God and those around us. I'm not so afraid of the aging process these days since I see it as making me a little more like Jesus before I go home. And like any refining process at the hands of a loving God, I can either cooperate with the plan or kick and scream as the Master refines me for my own benefit and the benefit of those around me. There is pain in this life. I hope we can learn to let pain be our guide.

Pain in the World

One of the questions I needed answered, like most people, was why there was so much pain in the world if our God was supposed to be a loving God. Here is how He has helped me to understand this. Pain in the body is something no one wants to experience, but it's actually beneficial to us. If we didn't experience pain, we wouldn't understand there is something wrong in the body and that we need to see a physician.

In like manner, there is pain in the world. This pain is an indicator that something is wrong in the body of humanity and that we need to see a physician. God has been referred to as the "Great Physician." Just as pain is an indicator that something is wrong in the body, God has allowed (not caused) pain in the world to indicate that something is wrong. Hospital wall boards show the level of the patients' pain from zero to ten to show anyone entering the room how bad their pain level is. Earthly pain is the direct result of our choosing what Satan would want us to choose rather than what God would want us to choose. Look closely at the words of Jesus Christ in what we have termed the Lord's Prayer in Matthew 6:13. "But deliver us from the evil one." This evil one is Satan, who directly opposes choices made that would honor God, each other, and ourselves. The Greek word used here for "evil" is *poneros*. Here is how *HELPS Word-studies* describes *poneros*:

4190 *ponērós* (an adjective which is also used substantively, derived from 4192 /*pónos*, "pain, laborious trouble") – properly, *pain-ridden*, emphasizing the inevitable agonies (misery) that always go with *evil.*[6]

It seems like Jesus is telling us that pain is a direct result of not making proper, loving choices. There are different levels of pain in this world that should indicate to us the level of pain sin, the missing of marks, is causing in our world. One of the hardest ideas to process was that of the pain of innocent children being abused in different ways and why God would allow such things to exist. And while we blame such things on God for allowing them to exist, the truth is that He has given us everything we need as a society to keep such things from happening, but many of us reject His truth, and all of us have turned our backs on Him at times.

Pain in this world is an indicator that something is wrong and that we need to go see the "Physician." Pain exists because we as a people haven't learned how to love God with all our hearts, souls, and minds; and love others as ourselves. The natural order of things has changed (nature). We have exchanged what is natural for what is unnatural, and we see the effects of this change in the nature of all things in this world. And we accept much of the unnatural as natural now because we are becoming so accustomed to it. I do believe that if every person turned to God to begin learning how to love from the mind (agape) and heart (phileo) appropriately and made Godly choices, we would see the world's pain subside. God will always do what is best for mankind while giving us the gift of free choice. But He will

---

[6] *HELPS Word-studies* taken from *The Discovery Bible* software, available at thediscoverybible.com, copyright © 2018, HELPS Ministries Inc. Used by permission. All rights reserved.

also not stop loving us in a way that is best for us, which means allowing painful circumstances in this world so we can see the consequences of sinful choices. And maybe someday the pain in the world will direct us back to Him.

If there were no pain in the world, we probably wouldn't see our need to return to Him. The loving thing for a God who loves us and gives us free will is to allow pain to exist, so we will see what separation from Him causes. And we will return to the one who can heal all pain and right any wrong. Please understand that it is not necessarily our personal sin that brings pain, though often this is the case, but because we live in a broken world full of sin, missing the mark of the way God wants us to Love Him, others and ourselves. Jesus, who was innocent, chose to suffer on our behalf, because of us missing the mark. When we accept our part in suffering on behalf of others in this world, doesn't that make us a little more like Him? With all that said, God is still very active in our circumstances, especially as we invite Him into them. He wants to be our healer, and when He allows pain in our world, He wants to be our comforter. No matter what happens in our circumstances, please remember these verses:

> Now to him who is able to do immeasurably more than all we ask or imagine, according to his power that is at work within us. (Ephesians 3:20)

> For I am convinced that neither death nor life, neither angels nor demons, neither the present nor the future, nor any powers, neither height nor depth, nor anything else in all creation, will be able to separate us from the Love of God that is in Christ Jesus our Lord. (Romans 8:38–39)

God is always with us, even in the painful circumstances He allows. And the following is what we have to look forward to as His children. Revelation 21:3–4 says, "And I heard a loud voice from the throne saying, 'Look! God's dwelling place is now among the people, and he will dwell with them. They will be his people, and God himself will be with them and be their God. He will wipe every tear from their eyes. There will be no more death or mourning or crying or pain, for the old order of things has passed away.'"

Sometimes we just need to hang on for His promises to be revealed. In the meantime, He is in it with us to heal, comfort, and give us the power and strength we need to endure while He seeks to bring others to Himself and conform His children to the image of His Son, Jesus Christ. But there are also times when we just drift in the stream of His joy and blessings, thanking Him for the pleasant moments in life and reaching out to help those who are experiencing pain. Which of the following statements do you believe to be true about our God?

- God is more interested in changing your circumstances so you will be okay.
- God is more interested in changing you so you will be okay in any circumstance.

We live in a broken world, and the more we become like Jesus, the more we understand this world and are willing to take our part in the suffering and healing that help us to identify with Him and His plan to redeem humanity. If we weren't broken, there would be nothing to redeem. He allows our brokenness and meets us in the middle of it. I will continue to age and watch the world be stripped away from me. I am willing to go through this process, which shows the world its dire need for someone to heal the pain. If that is my part in loving this world with agape love, then I ask God to be merciful to me and for His will to be done. And I pray that you will make it your life's goal to seek after loving God with all your heart, soul, and mind; and to love others as yourself.

In Christ's love,

Bibliography

Bible Hub © 2004 – 2016 by Bible Hub. Biblehub.net.

Chapman, Gary. The Five Love Languages: How to Express Heartfelt Commitment to Your Mate. Northfield Publishing. 1995

HELPS Word-studies taken from The Discovery Bible software, available at thediscoverybible.com, copyright © 2018, HELPS Ministries Inc. Used by permission. All rights reserved.

Keating, Thomas. The Human Condition: Contemplation and Transformation. Snowmass, CO: St. Benedict's Monastery, 1999.

St. John of The Cross, "Dark Night of The Soul," CCEL.org website and special contents copyright (1993-2015) Harry Plantinga

Strong, James. Strong's Exhaustive Concordance S.T.D., LL.D. 1890 Public Domain

Willard, Dallas. Renovation Of The Heart, Putting On The Character Of Christ. Colorado Springs, Co, NavPress © 2002.